What is network marketing all about?

Why is it making so many people wealthy?

Is it ethical?

Is it going to last?

All these questions, and many more, are answered in...

BOOM BUSINESS OF THE 90's

This easy-to-read, informative introduction to network marketing shows exactly how anyone can start their own low-risk, low-cost business – with the potential of making a fortune.

Top earners in the business have given the book unstinted praise:

Brilliantly simple . . . gives all the basics for sucess – Geoff Liberman.

By far the best introduction to the subject. Start reading, and you won't be able to put it down... – Shay O'Brien.

ABOUT THE AUTHOR

Francis Hitching has been writing books, magazine and newspaper articles, and television programmes all his working life.

After a successful career in Fleet Street, he moved to TV where he originated and produced the legendary pop programme *Ready, Steady, Go!*

His first book, *Earth Magic,* was an inquiry into the origins of Stonehenge and other megalithic monuments. He wrote and produced a major TV documentary based on its findings.

His international best-seller, *The World Atlas of Mysteries,* sold more than 300,000 copies in the UK alone. Many of the topics were adapted and produced by him for the award winning TV series *In Search Of...,* narrated by Leonard Nimoy, which was shown in 22 countries and is still being aired in the United States.

His account of the debate about Darwinism, *The Neck of the Giraffe,* was chosen as Book of the Year by the Novel prize winner William Golding, and by the acclaimed novelist John Updike. It was selected as Book of the Month by Reader's Digest, and was also serialized in Life Magazine. A two-part BBC–TV documentary based on it, and narrated by him, is used in the A–level biology curriculum in English schools.

Francis Hitching's gift as a documentary writer is to go the heart of a complex subject and make it plain and readable. In *Boom Business of the 90's,* a balanced account of network marketing's success story, he gives the crucial information for anyone new to the subject.

BOOM BUSINESS OF THE 90's

THE ESSENTIAL START–UP GUIDE TO NETWORK MARKETING

by Francis Hitching

MPG PUBLICATIONS

Published in Great Britain by
MPG Publications
for the Manchester Premier Group
29 The Downs, Altrincham, Cheshire WA14 2QD

To order this book telephone: 061–881–4134

First published in 1992

British Library Cataloguing in Publication Data – A catalogue record for this book is available from the British Library.

ISBN 0–9519442–0–7

Text processing and typesetting by PanSet Arts, Idenden House, Medway Street, Maidstone, Kent, ME14 1JT.

Cover Design by Tony Stocks Graphics, London, W1N 7RE.

Printed and bound in Great Britain by Mackays of Chatham, PLC.

CONTENTS

ACKNOWLEDGEMENTS

The most successful people in network marketing are those who have the skill, energy, and patience to teach others. I am fortunate that so many of them gave up time to me. For an overview of the industry, I was helped greatly by Richard Berry of the Direct Selling Association, and Andrew Hughes-Hallett, Director of the Multi-Level Marketing International Association.

For their views on the industry from the standpoint of their particular company, I thank (in alphabetical order) Stuart Birt, Shaun Charity, Richard Hobby, David Hooker, Geoffrey Jago, Nigel Swabey, Alec Waterman, and Martin Williams.

When it came to looking at the activities of a company in detail, I chose National Safety Associates of America. Its managing director in the UK, Ken Sellers, gave me encouragement and careful advice. Its many distributors in the field provided me with both information and inspiration. Chief among them were Geoff Liberman and Shay O'Brien, who spent endless hours making sure I understood the nuances and ethics of the business.

Others provided valuable help, too, and I list them with gratitude: Len Abel, Lee Allen, Brian Anderson, Ron Brand, Larry Brooks, Gary Chamberlain, Gary Crane, Shami Dhillon, Charlie Elliott, Duncan Gray, Nigel How, David Hunt, Jean and Yan Jovanovic, Bert Jukes, Zoe Kent, Mo Khan, Alex MacPhail, Bob Middleton, Jim Quinn, Vivienne and Derek Ross, David and Lynn Selwood, David Sherman and Richard Steele.

And last but not least, my lovely daughter who accompanied me and supported me as I searched my way through the subject.

Emma, this is for you.

INTRODUCTION

I was introduced to network marketing by my accountant in 1991.

Try it – I think you'll like it, he said.

He knew that documentary TV and publishing, the businesses where I and many of my friends regularly earn our living, were in the doldrums. ITV franchises were up for sale, advertising revenue was down, and hardly any programmes were being commissioned. Publishing, after profligate years in the 1980s, was shedding staff and slashing the level of advances for new books.

Network marketing seems recession proof, said my accountant. *It's booming. Go and see what's happening.*

So I did. And I was amazed. At the first meeting I went to, in Birmingham, there were several hundred people, most of them, like myself, taking a bewildered first look. Later, at other meetings round the country, there were audiences ranging from fifty to two thousand or more. At first glance, the business seemed almost too good to be true. For everywhere the message was the same.

On to the platforms came speaker after speaker telling how their lives had been transformed because they had grasped the opportunity that network marketing offered them.

I remember hearing Geoff Liberman tell how, two years earlier, he decided he had had enough of working as a dance instructor in Manchester. Now he was travelling the world, with a business turning over several hundred thousand pounds a month. He drew little circles and connecting lines to show how his business had multiplied by the power of geometrical progression.

I remember, too, the impression left by Derek and Vivienne Ross, a husband-and-wife team who, in about the same period of time, had come from the brink of financial disaster to a position of such security that they could now stop work, if they chose to.

But above all I remember the buzz. Quite clearly, something extraordinarily powerful was going on. At a time when the country as a whole was deeply depressed, here was a group of people with no common background saying: *Come on, join in. There's a new life to be had. This business is simple and rewarding – and we'll give you all the help you want.*

The concept hooked me at once. By my whole career has taught me to check out testimony that sounds a bit glib, to be wary of mass movements, and to ask: what's the catch? I picked up and scanned what literature there was, and found it mostly American in tone, to my eyes overloaded with motivational hype.

Then, as I went round the meetings, I met some of the major players in network marketing, and talked to them at length. One, Shay O'Brien, introduced me to the person I had first heard speak: Geoff Liberman. When they found I was an author, they encouraged me to write on network marketing as I saw it – as an outsider reporting the situation objectively, warts and all. They were confident that if I looked at it in depth, I would see the enormous potential for people to start their own business, and become as wealthy as they had.

This book is the result. Lots of people, like me, are going to be enthusiastically introduced to network marketing over the next few years, and told it is the opportunity of a lifetime.

I believe now, after much research, that this is true. So what's it all about? Why isn't it better known? I hope this book will tell you. It's what I would like to have read the day after I went to my first meeting.

– Francis Hitching, Banbury, Oxon, 1992

Chapter 1

Too good to be true?

Wendy Williams is an outgoing mother of two teenage boys who lives in west London, and whose brown eyes shine with enthusiasm when she starts talking about what she is doing nowadays.

Two years ago, her life was in ruins.

Her husband Harry had just died tragically in a road accident. The other driver involved, who was to blame, was uninsured. Harry had been a computer consultant, running his own one-man business, and had borrowed from the bank to get things going. Their house was security against the loan.

The bank waited for what they regarded as a "decent interval" before moving in. The decent interval was just four months. Wendy Williams remembers how she opened the letter, and felt hope draining from her as she read it.

"It was abrupt, legal, final, and dreadful. I had to find the money within 90 days, or my house would be auctioned. The boys and I would have nowhere to live, and no income to live on.

"I couldn't even take it in properly to begin with. I was too much in a state of shock even to try.

"But they meant it all right. The house was possessed and put up for sale, and the bit of money I had left went towards renting a two-up, two-down. I didn't have the faintest idea what to do with my life. I still hadn't come to terms with being on my own."

Her friends rallied round, and invited her to see them as often as possible. And it was one of these who gave her the lifeline she needed.

"He was pretty successful in his job, something I don't quite understand in the City, but he'd heard of this way you could earn money in your spare time by inviting your friends to build up a network of people all sharing a range of environmentally-friendly products.

"He wasn't strapped for money like I was, but his bonuses from his regular job were nothing like they had been, and he seemed to be finding it really easy to replace them from his new networking business, with something to spare.

"He didn't tell me much about it, but suggested we went somewhere one evening where we could meet some other people all doing the same thing. I didn't need much persuading – it was an outing, apart from anything else.

"Anyway, the result was that although I wasn't at all convinced to begin with, I got involved. Really, I had nothing to lose, except the cost of a bit of product, which they said they would help find buyers for.

"I trusted him, because he was an old friend, and it's worked out perfectly. I rang up a few of my own friends and told them what I was doing, and whether it was out of pity to begin with or not, they joined in too, and soon found they were making money themselves.

"The more people who got involved, the more money I made, and the more they made. I can't describe what a wonderful feeling it gave me. I had something to think about and aim for, and every week I was meeting new people and having a social life instead of being stuck on my own moping.

"Honestly, I think it saved my life."

By January, 1992, Wendy Williams had more than 100 people in her network, and her cheque that month from the company she had joined was £2,816.00.

Like everyone else invited to take a look at network marketing for the first time, she found some large claims being made for it.

"I don't blame anyone for being sceptical," she says. "We all are, to begin with."

A business revolution

Network marketing is said – for instance, by Lord William Rees-Mogg, former editor of *The Times*, in his book *The Great Reckoning* – to be the next revolution in how to do business; it will boom while High Street retailing declines.

Success stories abound: stories of companies which have adopted the system and are now turning over hundreds of £ millions a year; of individuals who have made enough money to retire after only two or three years; of thousands of others who have freed themselves from financial worries for the first time in their lives.

Yet, in the UK business world, network marketing is only just surfacing. And for many who have distantly heard about it, it carries a dubious reputation.

It's a pyramid, chain-letter thing, isn't it?

It's all about wives drinking coffee and selling each other household stuff, isn't it?

There used to be some truth in both. About 20 years ago, dishonest pyramid salesmen found a way of attaching themselves to network marketing, which in itself is an entirely ethical business concept. Amid much publicity, legislation made it impossible for the fraud to continue – but the memory lingers on.

Historically, too, network marketing began in a small way through the sharing of vitamin products among friends. But today, big business has taken up the idea, and is encouraging anyone who would like to have an extra profit centre, or is thinking of a career change that might lead to serious wealth, to take a closer look at what's happening. Worldwide, including the UK, network marketing has defied recession, and is currently doubling in size every three or four years. Individual companies are doing even better than this.

Look beyond the history and the hype, and you will find it is a major international business. According to statis-

AND FATHER JOINED TOO

Shay O'Brien went into network marketing in April 1989, aged 25. Three years later, his network numbers thousands and turns over more than £1 million per month.

My father was managing director of a Jardine Matheson subsidiary, and saw me as following in his footsteps and eventually having a seat on the Board.

He was worried when I told him I was going into network marketing, because he was sure it would turn out to be a pyramid scam under another name. But I'd made up my mind, talked to him, and handed in my notice.

It took me a few months before it began to pay off. But then the company cheques started rolling in, and soon I was earning more than he was. He was amazed how quickly I had built a successful business, generating a passive income that is a permanent financial asset.

I think that's what he really envied. At Jardines, however hard he worked, he was not entitled to any equity. After 18 months, aged 55, he resigned to do the same as me. Today, he has his own solid business. He will go on earning through his group even if he stops work tomorrow – which he won't, because he enjoys it.

tics produced by the Direct Selling Association, it will achieve global sales of £7–8 billion in 1992. It may well be the most effective method yet invented of moving product from manufacturer to consumer.

Those involved have found that it has unique attractions:

ANYONE CAN PROFIT FROM NETWORK MARKETING, BECAUSE:

* You don't have to sell
* You can do it part-time
* You don't need special skills (but you need to be teachable)

ANYONE CAN START THEIR OWN LOW-RISK BUSINESS, BECAUSE:

* You don't need a big investment
* Your overheads will be virtually nil
* You don't employ staff (and you don't have a boss)
* You can make immediate income
* You learn the business while you earn

THE POTENTIAL IS LIMITLESS, BECAUSE:

* The more you learn and teach, the more people will succeed alongside you
* Your organisation can grow as large as you choose
* The bigger your organisation grows, the more money everyone makes

Now if you are hearing about networking for the first time, these are large claims. Particularly when you may also be told that for 5–15 hours per week part-time, you can make £5–20,000 profit per year. And that, full-time, there is no reason why you shouldn't make the same amount *per month*. Since the average annual wage in the UK is £12–15,000, and nobody except a few entrepreneurs, company chairmen, and TV presenters seem to make monthly figures in this range, it would be surprising if you didn't raise an eyebrow in disbelief.

But the fact is that the success stories are true. I have talked to more than a hundred people with incomes to prove it: students, teachers, secretaries, housewives;

"P.O.M., P.O.T."

Lee Allen, from Tynside, was in his early thirties when he was first invited to join network marketing.

I turned down the opportunity three times before deciding to make a career move. I had built up an insurance business which was bringing me in about £20,000 a month in commissions. That's a lot of income by any standards – particularly for someone like me who had started life as a blue-collar steelworker and been made redundant.

What made him change his mind was "P.O.M., P.O.T.".

I had plenty of money – but I didn't have the other half of being successful, which is plenty of time to enjoy it. I realised that if I wanted to go on earning that sort of money in financial services, I was on a treadmill. If I left my business for even a week, it began to distintegrate.

But with network marketing, most of what you earn comes from the work of other people you have taught.

So I launched myself into it – and made all the usual early mistakes. But three years on, I have more than replaced my income. And I can go on holiday as often as I like.

people who have been made redundant, or whose businesses have failed, or who have successfully sold up what they were doing to get in on the opportunity; bankers, accountants, doctors, dentists, nurses; builders, shopfloor workers, managers, salespeople – all these and many more.

There seems no common denominator except the general rule that *anyone can learn to do it.*

And because network marketing is relatively undeveloped in the UK and in Europe, for at least the next decade there will be an unparalleled opportunity for tens of thousands of new people to benefit.

Time and energy

Nobody who presents you with an honest picture of network marketing will pretend that achieving such results is easy, let alone automatic. It means setting up a distribution network in which a large number of people do a little each. That takes time and energy.

But there are huge advantages, one of which is that you choose who you want to work with. All you do is find a handful of friends, colleagues, or business associates who you feel would like the opportunity to distribute a range of products you all believe to be worthwhile. Then they in turn find some more people to do the same thing. Gradually (or quite quickly, if you work hard) the number of distributor levels will grow. Earlier names for network marketing (still used by some companies) were "multi-level" marketing, and "flex-marketing".

Before long, you will find yourself with an organisation of hundreds, or even thousands, of people like yourself. As a reward for having worked hard, and helping these people, the company will pay you, monthly, a percentage commission on group turnover.

It's not difficult – and certainly not expensive – to get started. You don't need a lot of capital, as you would if you were buying a franchise or setting up a traditional business.

You will make some money from the beginning: *learn as you earn*, the saying goes. Secondary incomes of £500 – £1,000 per month are common.

After that, it takes time, patience, understanding, teaching, and enthusiasm to lead your organisation into a significant size – just the same as building any business. Above all, it takes persistence. There is a significant drop-out rate from those who become disheartened by slow results. Inevitably, some such people will be in your organisation, and you will have to work to make sure you give them the help they need.

But the pot of gold is there for those who keep at it. Any established network marketing company can provide documentary evidence that their top earners, after two or three years in the business, are making more than £100,000 a year – in many cases, several times that.

Network marketing is about making dreams come true. You can dream about getting yourself out of a financial hole; or about buying the house or car or boat you always wanted; or not having to commute; or not having a boss; or having enough money to stop work altogether in 3-5 years' time. You can dream of developing enough self-confidence to take charge of your life, and not be dependent on others.

Successful people in network marketing – and there are tens of thousands of them – have achieved all this, and more.

Their guiding principle is so profoundly simple that you can only wonder why it's not better known:

YOU CAN MAKE A LIVING MARKETING A PRODUCT. BUT YOU CAN MAKE A FORTUNE BY BUILDING A NETWORK AND TEACHING OTHERS TO DO THE SAME.

Chapter 2

2 + 3 = 781

The purpose of network marketing is the same as with any other method of marketing: to distribute as much product as possible from the manufacturer to the end-user. Network marketing is growing explosively because, with the right products, companies are finding it does the job so well.

Here, typically, is why:

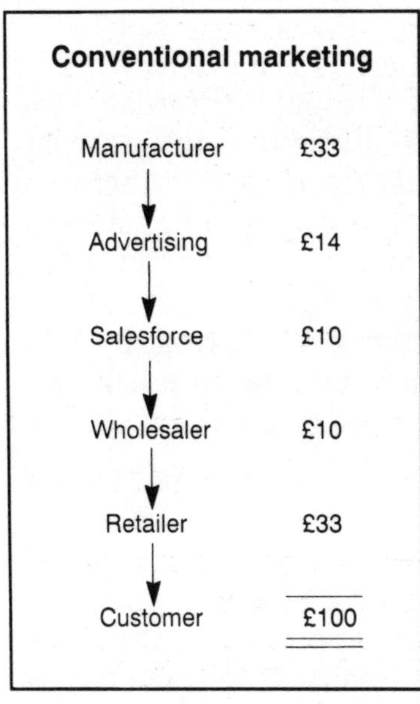

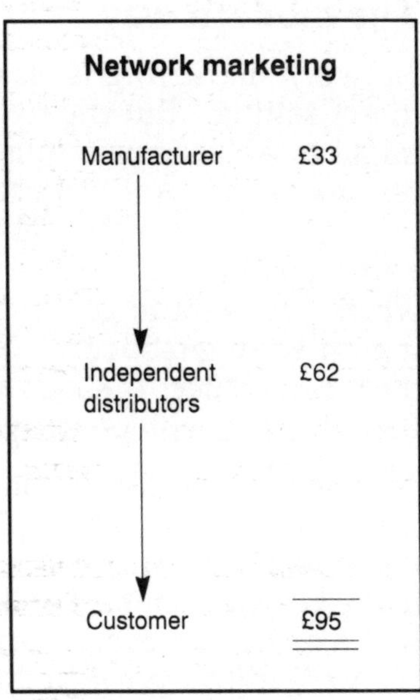

The MANUFACTURER is happy because he has simplified all his middleman costs; and as an even bigger bonus, has replaced his most unreliable cost, advertising, with the word-of-mouth recommendation of independent distributors running their own businesses.

The DISTRIBUTOR is happy because the rewards (and they're not just financial rewards) are potentially far higher than in a traditional marketing setup.

The CUSTOMER is happy because the product is good value, comes recommended by a friend, and can often be tried out at home before buying.

As the group marketing manager of US Sprint put it (US Sprint was a small company that used networking to compete with the telecommunications giant AT&T in a David-and-Goliath trade battle, and won):

Network marketing is the most powerful way yet found of putting the product in front of the consumer.

The modern way

Network marketing is classified as a modern form of direct selling. But the two are hugely different. You might as well compare riding a bike with driving the latest model car. And it's not just the difference between pedal power, where you have to do everything yourself, and a combustion engine which takes you smoothly where you want to go. In direct selling, you are knocking on strangers' doors. Network marketing, by contrast, is a contact business where you get in touch on a friendly basis with people you already know.

So independent distributors are not encouraged to consider themselves salespeople. However, it is helpful to know that most sizeable network marketing companies in the UK are members of the Direct Selling Association, which operates a code of practice approved by the Office of Fair Trading. When you are invited to become part of network marketing, it is worth asking whether the company concerned is a member of the DSA. If so, its system will have been thoroughly vetted.

Network marketing is also one of the few business methods so far discovered where you can *only* become wealthy by helping others to become wealthy too. It happens through the process of DUPLICATION.

Duplication

You will find the word duplication coming up again and again in network marketing. It is central to the whole business of building a business, and teaching others how to do the same. You duplicate your efforts; you duplicate your teaching methods; and the people you sponsor duplicate what you have taught them to do.

Mathematically, it is known as geometric progression. It has awesome power. If, on the first day of the month, you put 1p in a piggy bank, and the following day 2p, and the third day 4p, and so on until the end of the month – how much money would you have at the end of 30 days? £1,000? £10,000?

In fact, the answer is: more than £5 million.

And even though in real life nothing turns out to be as perfect as this, the principle of building a network is just as simple. You sponsor two people, those two people sponsor two more, and those four sponsor two each to make eight...

It's not very different from a family tree, where a couple get together and form the beginnings of a new lineage. By the time the third or fourth generation has been reached, the number of cousins and in-laws can be 50 or more.

In a rudimentary form, the idea of duplication was first applied to business about 50 years ago. It came about because direct selling has a built-in problem. Suppose a company hires a salesman to open up a new territory. Working maybe 12 hours a day, he begins to do really well. Great, the company thinks – let's put in another salesman, and we'll make twice as many sales.

But how does the first salesman feel about this? Not good. He's had his territory carved up, he's in competition with someone new, sales are harder to make, and he's already working all the hours he can stay awake. So he ups and leaves to sell another product for someone else.

Networking begins

It was the US company California Vitamins, in the 1940's, which first found a way of resolving this. It decided to give the salesman a reward if he could generate new business in his territory through bringing in other people to help him. He received a bonus for each new person he sponsored, or helped to introduce, and also a small commission on the increased turnover. Suddenly, the salesman was happy again. Even if he brought in only two new people, and others did the same, this is what happened:

LEADER	1st level	Total	1
× 2			+
2	2nd level		2
× 2			+
4	3rd level		4
× 2			+
8	4th level		8
× 2			+
16	5th level		16
	Total:		31

California Vitamins could hardly believe their luck. Previously, the salesman on his own had moved product worth, say, $200 a month (remember, it was the 1940s).

Now, through encouraging him to duplica
they had a turnover of 31 × $200 = $6,200.

But this was only the beginning. People began to realise that if they sponsored just one more person, and taught everyone to do the same, the power of geometric progression would give their group far more strength in numbers.

They didn't even have to work much harder to do it. Instead of starting with two people, they started with three, and taught these three how to sponsor three more, and so on down the line.

But if the difference at the beginning was only one extra new person, look at what happened after five levels:

LEADER	1st level	Total	1
× 3			+
3	2nd level		3
× 3			+
9	3rd level		9
× 3			+
27	4th level		27
× 3			+
81	5th level		81
	Total:		121

Even if the average amount of product moved by each person was halved, at $100, the monthly turnover was now tremendous: $121,000. Yet all leader had done was find one extra person in the first month, and taught others to do the same.

Growing by word of mouth

Around this time, in the natural course of events, other things happened to network marketing. Firstly the distributors, because of the large numbers needed, stopped being the exclusive preserve of male door-knockers working in their own territory. Instead, it became an army of part-timers looking for some extra income. And because of the nature of California Vitamin's products, these now included many women.

Secondly – and just as important – these women found they were able to earn good money not from selling on the road, as their husbands had been doing, but simply from sharing with friends what California Vitamins had to offer. At coffee mornings all over the west coast of America, women were introduced to California Vitamins, decided they liked it, and began to form networks of their own.

This word-of-mouth recommendation from friend to friend marked the true birth of network marketing. And almost simultaneously, a third thing happened: some people began to get very wealthy indeed.

Finding five

Again, it had to do with the power of numbers. Whereas the full-time salesmen might have had difficulty finding even two good fellow-salesmen prepared to switch jobs, almost everybody has more than two friends who want to make a bit of extra money. It became the goal of the new breed of network marketers to multiply themselves by 5.

Today, that is the norm. Five levels times 5 people is the total you will be encouraged to aim for. And even though the numbers may look extraordinarily large, the law of geometrical progression is so powerful that they happen.

Because all you have done is find five people in the first

place, instead of two or three – and taught others to do the same:

LEADER	1st level	Total	1
× 5			+
5	2nd level		5
× 5			+
25	3rd level		25
× 5			+
125	4th level		125
× 5			+
625	5th level		625
	Total:		781

California Vitamins found, of course, that it took longer for networks to build to this level than the first 2 × 2 format. But so what? At the end of it, if everyone averaged even a $50 product order, monthly turnover was $390,000 – an annual rate approaching $5 million.

Yet all that had happened, to change the network size from 31 to 781, was for the original person to share California Vitamins with five people instead of two – and teach them and their five people to do the same.

As a California Vitamins executive put it to a group of successful women: *Ladies, you have invented a new concept of mathematics. You have proved to me that the difference between 31 and 781 is 3!*

The reward factor

Now, imagine the position of the original salesman, who would probably have left the company if California Vitamins hadn't devised their new reward system.

With a turnover in his group of around $5,000,000 a year, his 2% commission was earning him $100,000. And he wasn't even having to work the 12 hours a day that he used to. He could take holidays – a month, two months – and his group would still turn over almost exactly the same amount, because he was only one of 781.

What's more, people were happy and non-competitive. The normal cut-throat corporate climb to the top had been turned on its head. Look at these two diagrams. On the left is the shape of a typical company, with 625 people at its lowest level of management, all hoping to climb the ladder to become managing director. At each level, there is only one promotion for every five people. Competition between colleagues is fierce and unending.

On the right is how network marketing shapes up. The more people who come in, the better it is for everyone. Instead of competing, you teach how to succeed. The more, the merrier. It is a revolutionary business concept.

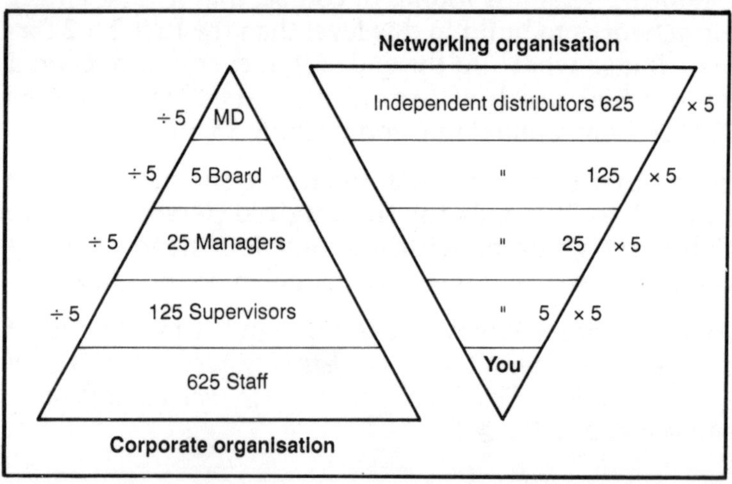

By the end of the 1960s, network marketing had become an established part of the American business system, and was expanding to other countries as well. Everything seemed set fair – until pyramids suddenly got themselves a bad name.

Chapter 3

Networking ethics

The pyramid scams lasted only a few years, in the early 1970s, before they were made illegal in the US, the UK, and most countries on the continent of Europe. They were totally different from network marketing, which is designed to provide longterm benefits with the same rules for all. Instead, they were get-rich-if-you-can-and-get-out-quick schemes for the cowboys of this world.

Only those at or very near the top of the pyramid ever made any money. Typically, the cowboy who started the scheme would print some glossy brochures singing the praises of a new product which "could not fail" to sell. If the product existed (it often didn't), he made sure enough was available at rock-bottom prices for him to start a distribution chain.

Then a vicious game of pass-the-parcel began. The rules were usually something like this:

Misusing the power of geometric progression, he carved up a territory into five regions, and found five people willing to pay him an entry fee of several thousand pounds for exclusive distribution rights in each region. He also sold them – at a profit – as much product as he could talk them into.

Now it was the turn of these five people to find five more people, each with a smaller distribution area. Again, they were charged an entrance fee, and paid a bumped-up price for the parcel of product which had been passed on to them.

And so it went on, with an ever-larger number of people paying an entrance fee for an ever-smaller area, buying product at an ever-higher price. Quite soon in the pyramid, the cost of the product went way past its true retail value, and thousands of victims were left with garages full of unsaleable, over-priced stock.

Today, the differences with network marketing seem obvious. In pyramid schemes, there was no fixed wholesale price: it depended on what level of the pyramid you joined. There was often no company with which to have a contract, and therefore no buy-back guarantee. On top of that, there was a requirement to pay a large entrance fee and buy a fixed amount of product, which it was your responsibility to get rid of.

If you didn't, you were stuck with what you bought.

Pyramids made illegal

In spite of all these disadvantages, unscrupulous operators still found it possible to present pyramids as an easy way of getting rich quickly, and a lot of people were taken in. So in the 1970s, here and in the US, laws were passed to protect the unsuspecting.

Exorbitant entry fees were banned (the UK maximum is now £75, and most companies charge much less than this). A written contract, with a number of strict conditions, had to exist between the company and the independent distributor. Distributors could cancel the contract without penalty. In the UK, saleable product must be bought back by the company at 90% of the price paid for it.

Above all, product had to exist, and the main purpose of any network marketing scheme should be to distribute the product to a genuine end-user.

The legislation did nothing but good. The cowboys moved on to other fields. Reputable network marketing companies had their activities legitimised – particularly after 1979, when Amway's method of trading was tested in US courts, and given a clean bill of health.

The result was that network marketing began to mushroom. Throughout the difficult years of the pyramid scams, about 30 companies had kept going. Now they were joined, first by a few dozen, then by hundreds. A common vocabulary emerged:

SPONSOR: (As a verb) – find new distributors for your network, and teach them the business. (As a noun) – the person who introduced you to the programme, and is responsible for helping you in the early stages, so long as you put in the effort.

SHARE: Show the product to someone, with a view to him or her buying it, and/or becoming a distributor.

UPLINE: Your sponsor, your sponsor's sponsor, and so on all the way up to the company you have joined.

DOWNLINE: Everyone in your group who joined after you.

LEG (or LINE): A part of your group that starts with someone personally sponsored by you.

PURCHASE VOLUME (or PV): The total amount of orders put in to the company by you and your group in a given period.

LEVEL/GENERATION: Easier to draw than describe. This is how three levels (of three each) looks:

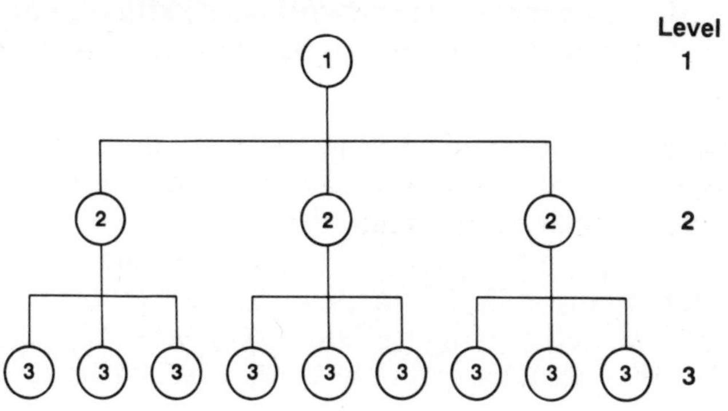

By the mid 1980s the number of network marketing companies in the US had grown from 30 to more than 1,000, and newly-signed independent distributors were coming in at the rate of at least one million a year.

The corporate bandwagon

What all these companies cottoned on to was that if they built up a large number of self-motivated, self-replicating independent distributors, and kept them happy by rewarding them for the amount of effort they put in, good products found end-users almost automatically. The benefits of a networking operation were enormous:

* Low start-up costs
* Rapid expansion and market penetration
* Little or no expenditure on media advertising; instead, massive exposure by word of mouth

There was, of course, a huge dropout rate. Thousands of start-up businesspeople with a novel product thought they could make a fortune. Usually undercapitalized and unable to handle a distributor network, they vanished almost as fast as they arrived.

The crucial technological development that enabled the best companies to survive and thrive was growth in computer power. Many of the management problems stemmed from the fact that companies simply couldn't keep track of all the transactions and commissions due. Nowadays, every major network marketing company has a dedicated computer system which takes care of this.

The largest network marketing company in the world is Amway, formed by a breakaway management group formerly with California Vitamins. Worldwide, Amway's turnover exceeds $3 billion annually, and it has more than a million independent distributors to take care of. Gillette, Colgate-Palmolive, Mastercard, and many other major companies, now use, or have subsidiaries which use, a form of network marketing as a sales method.

By 1991, network marketing in the US, as monitored by the Direct Selling Association, accounted for sales of $6–7 billion a year – and the growth graph was still rising. When you include the sales figures of non-member companies, the total was perhaps $10–15 billion. And it wasn't just an all American success story.

Global growth

Globally, the Direct Sales Association estimates that direct selling in some form or other is a worldwide business in excess of £25 billion in 34 countries achieved by 9 million people. Network marketing's share of this may be about half.

In the Far East, it is thriving. In Japan, where retail premises in big cities cost a fortune, it is an obvious answer. Around 80% of Toyota's domestic sales – which involve a catalogue of products and services as well as cars – are achieved by independent distributors rewarded through the size of their network.

In Europe, too, it is becoming standard industry practice. Most of the major US networking companies have developed an operation in continental Europe. In the UK, the scene is similarly set for explosive growth. We're just as good at it. On average, the average UK network distributor moves about £1,500 worth of product a

Cracking the telephone monopoly

One of the most convincing examples of the power of network marketing as applied to big business came with the de-regulation of the US telecommunications industry in 1989. Two young companies, MCI and US Sprint, decided to attack the near-monopoly held by AT&T.

In a single year, AT&T lost 26% market share – and promptly formed a network marketing division itself.

year – the same as our counterparts in the US. The only difference is that the system has been operating over there longer.

UK network marketing is on target to reach US levels within the next five years, and when it does, it will be at least a £750m per year business.

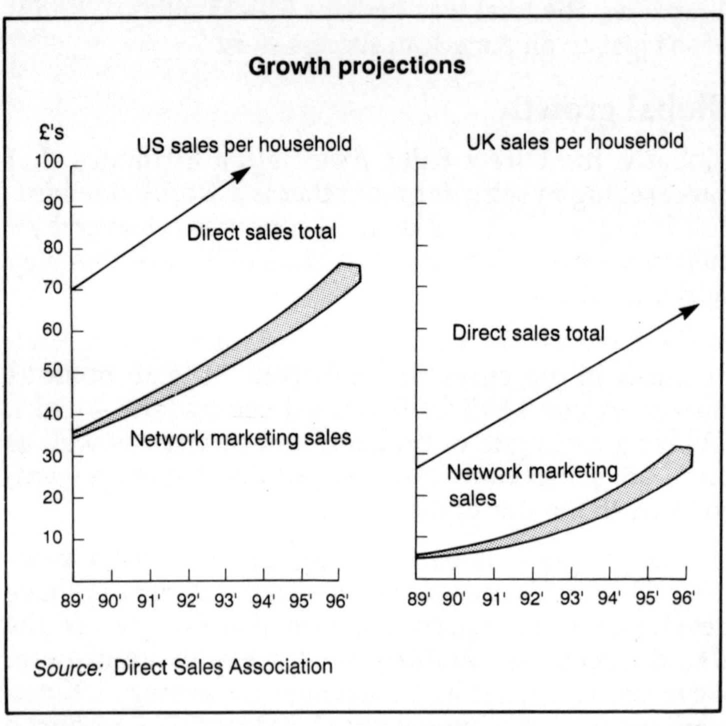

Source: Direct Sales Association

Analysis of the record of successful versus unsuccessful businesses shows that a network survives and prospers only if the company offers the distributor three guarantees.

First, the company will abide by an ethical principle:

1. EVERYONE IS ON AN EQUAL FOOTING

Meaning that: no matter when you join, and what place you are in the organisation, you have exactly the same opportunities as everyone else.

Of course, people who have been in the business longest, worked hardest, and have built the biggest networks, are bound to be making more money than you, when you begin.

But the rules make it perfectly possible – and quite usual – for late starters to overtake those who introduced them.

2. THE PRODUCTS ARE GOOD VALUE

Without exception, the track record of every networking company successful in the long term shows that it has a timely product priced to sell. If nobody buys, the network collapses. It's as straightforward as that.

But good value means something else as well: the products should always contain an automatic "repeat" element. That is to say, customers will re-order product as a matter of course. Repeat sales bring a passive income to distributors, so that they go on earning even when they're not working.

3. THE BUSINESS IS SIMPLE

When you are first confronted with a company's marketing plan – its particular way of rewarding its distributors – this may not seem to be so. You will very likely find a ladder of promotion that gives you a complex series of bonuses and percentage commissions depending on how much volume you and your network have achieved.

But virtually all these marketing plans are simple at heart. They offer rewards in three areas:

* RETAILING – you profit from an end-user buying your product.
* WHOLESALING – you profit from supplying your new people with inventory.
* NETWORKING – the company pays you a small percentage on your group's turnover.

If you're just starting, or if you're just looking for a bit of extra part-time income, most of your money will come from the first two activities.

But if you want to become a professional network marketer, and plan to build a full-time business, it is invariably the third aspect that generates the huge sums of money which some people are able to make. It is this small percentage, paid on the volume you have helped create through hundreds or thousands of people in your group, which in the end provides not just the six-figure annual profits, but the ability to retire on a passive income.

As John Paul Getty put it:

I would rather earn 1% of 100 people's effort, than 100% of my own.

Networking millionaires

For many, network marketing has paid off handsomely over the years. At least one person in the UK authentically earned more than £1 million in 1991, and hundreds earned well in excess of £100,000. Some published accounts claim that there are 100,000 $ millionaires in the US who have made their money through network marketing.

While this claim seems unrealistically high, it is certainly true that the potential earnings for ordinary people from network marketing are phenomenal – and everyone will have started in the same way, with a few good friends and a minimal amount of capital.

Peter Clothier, formerly of the UK's Trading Standards Office, has made a special study of the subject, and become a trusted authority. He has satisfied himself that it *has allowed hundreds of people worldwide to develop £1m p.a. incomes, and thousands more to reach millionaire status.*

Chapter 4

"You don't have to sell..."

At this point, in any study of network marketing, you come face to face with a big puzzle.

Clearly, the aim of the companies is to sell as much product as they possibly can. That's why they're using network marketing. It works. It moves product. It sells.

Yet you, the distributor, are told again and again: *you don't have to sell.*

How can this be? What's the answer?

It's an important issue, because at least 95% of us hate every aspect of selling, believe we're no good at selling, and especially dislike the idea of selling to friends.

It's also the main reason why people turn down the opportunity of profiting from network marketing. Most people, when they have been introduced to the opportunity properly, become enthusiastic very quickly.

OK, I appreciate it's not a pyramid.

Yes, it's obviously a fast-growing business.

Sure, I can see how you make money out of it.

Yes, I like the product.

Of course I know people who'd like to be better off.

BUT:

I'm sorry, I'd be hopeless at selling – let alone to my friends.

Which is a pity, because you truly do not have to "sell", in any sense of the word as we normally understand it.

If you want an answer to the puzzle, it lies in the nature of building a network. Look carefully at the section which follows. Network marketing is simple but revolutionary. And it is so different from any other "selling" concept you have come across before that it is bound to take time to sink in.

There are just four essential things you have to do – and keep on doing – if you want to lay down the foundations for a successful network marketing business. Not one of them involves the word "selling". These are what they are:

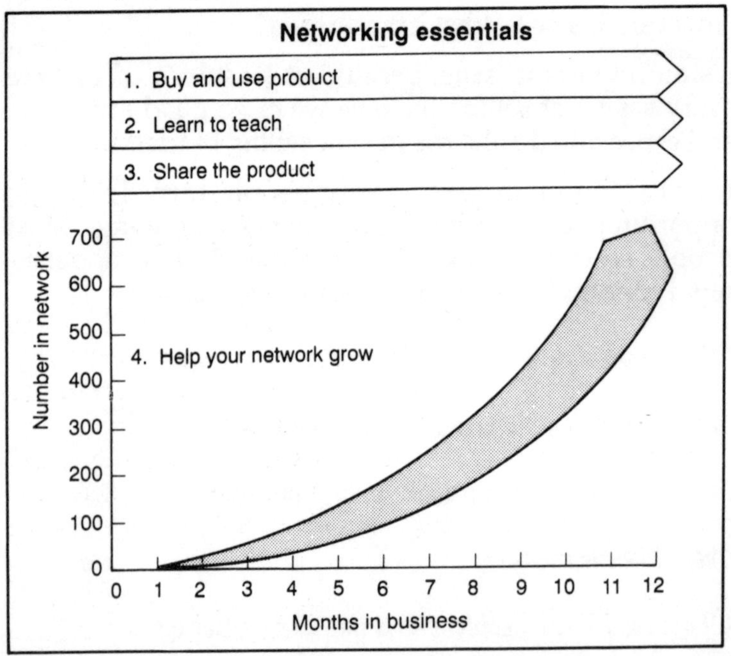

Let's look at these essentials in more detail. They are the

like the four cylinders in the new car you are driving. Keep them turning over, and the engine will get you smoothly where you want to go. Stop firing on any of them, and you will eventually stutter to a halt.

1. BUY AND USE SOME PRODUCTS

This is your starting point. By all means look around different network marketing possibilities before you reach for your cheque book, but to get moving there is only one thing to do: buy some products and use them.

If you don't, you won't begin to know what you're dealing with. And unless you like the product line, and have faith in it, you will be unconvincing when it comes to building a network. If you've chosen the right product, you will feel good about using it, and excited about its benefits to others. You will find yourself wanting to describe how well it works. And who will you tell first? Your family and friends, of course.

2. LEARN TO TEACH

Next, your aim is to build a circle of people as enthusiastic and committed as you. There are ways of doing this – and ways of putting people off. The next chapter will give you a few introductory pointers as to which ways work best.

To begin with, talk to your sponsor, and find out as much as possible about the business face to face. Remember that when you in turn share the opportunity with a friend, you will be asked the same questions. So listen to how your sponsor goes about answering them. You will learn the facts that explain your new business properly, and learn how scepticism is overcome – your own included.

Network marketing opens up genuine and unique possibilities for you to develop as a person and to build a sizeable business. It is simple in concept but sophisticated in practice. Nobody can expect to understand or appreciate its subtleties on day one. Whether you expect to earn an extra £10,000 a year, or £30,000, or £100,000, you can hardly expect to do it without putting yourself on a learning curve. And in network marketing, that means learning how to teach people to teach other people to do the same as you.

The whole of your first month can be regarded as an intensive training period. Certainly, you will earn as you learn. But if your business is to be long-lasting and successful, you absolutely have to become a teacher yourself. The better the networking company you choose, the more opportunities for training there will be. You should aim to become an even better teacher than the person who introduced you.

3. SHARE THE PRODUCT

This aspect of network marketing – sharing – is the closest you will come to selling. But you will find the two are very different.

"Selling", to most people, means persuading someone to buy something they neither need nor want, and probably can't afford anyway. "Selling", of this sort, is hostile, and unwelcome.

"Sharing", on the other hand, is entirely friendly. You share all sorts of things with friends and family: an experience, an opinion of a film or restaurant, a joke, books, magazines, a bit of DIY equipment, news, gossip, a holiday, bargains, opinions. It's part of civilized life. Sharing is simply day-to-day socialising.

And sharing is at the heart of network marketing. Anybody you talk to who becomes interested in the opportunity will automatically, just like yourself, want to try the product out and use it – without any further encouragement from you. Share it with them. Let them try it.

A number of companies offer gift introductory packs, or free trial use, of their products. This, too, is another way of sharing and discussing both the product and the business opportunity. If someone likes the product, but for any of a number of reasons doesn't want to join your network, the chances are that he or she will be a buyer. Excellent. You will have made a retail sale without even trying – by sharing.

Retailing is the key to getting your business started. When people buy product, you make an immediate profit. It's positive cash flow, as your bank manager or any businessperson will tell you. It introduces you to new people who may want to join your network. It provides end-users for the product, without whom the company would go out of business.

But even though you will find retailing gets easier the more you go along, you should still ration the time you spend on it. Because the final essential is:

4. HELP YOUR NETWORK GROW

Different sponsors will give you different guidelines on how you should divide your time between retailing and building your network. One sensible suggestion is that you should reckon, initially, on 40% retailing, 40% sharing the opportunity, and 20% on management and training. As time goes by, and you have a large network to look after, the retailing side will drop to 20% or even 10%.

Because you should always keep your ultimate goals in mind. You are looking towards changing your life. And you can only achieve this through teaching and motivating others to do the same as you. Provided you manage this, your network will grow eventually to such a size that you can achieve a six-figure passive income. Although this may take three to five years, the law of geometric progression will work in your favour in the end.

All this is not to say that people with sales skills – trained or natural – are unwelcome in network marketing. Some become outstandingly successful. But all of them have found that conventional sales techniques are largely irrelevant. Indeed, they can get in the way of progress.

Graphically, it is easy to see what happens if you spend too much time retailing. Your networking income never gets a chance to take off:

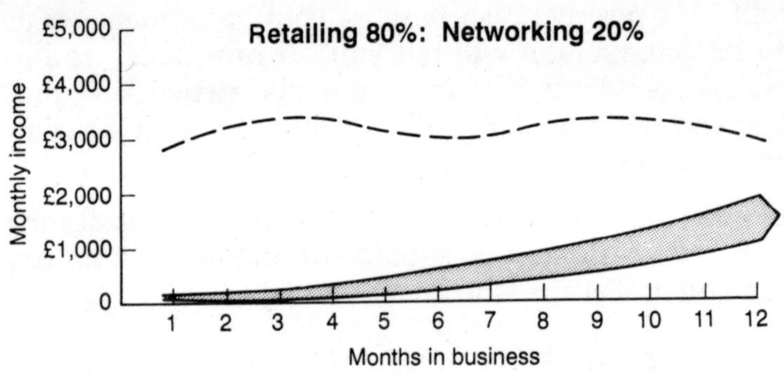

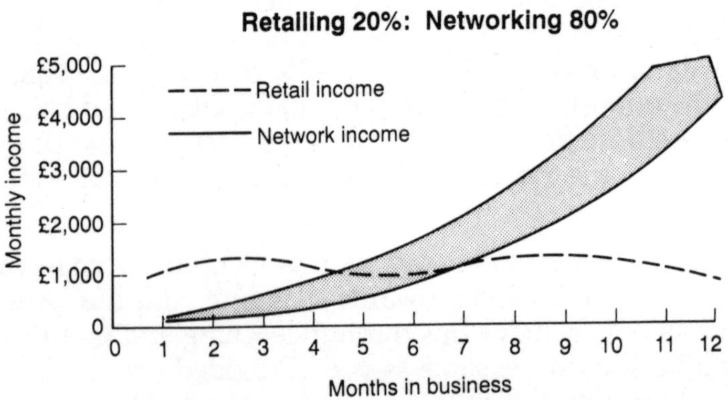

The trouble with salespeople is that this split goes against their instinct and training. Usually, their immediate reaction to the opportunity offered by network marketing is to jump in with both feet and either: (a)

sponsor as many people as possible; or (b), sell as much product as possible.

Either way will almost certainly bring headaches, or worse. Let's illustrate this with what happens, typically, to three different sorts of people coming into network marketing for the first time. For simplicity, we'll say they all have jobs bringing in about £1,500 a month, and see how well they do with their different approaches.

Salestype 1

The first person, *Salestype 1,* decides to sponsor like crazy. In spite of keeping going at her full-time job, she's so dynamic that she sponsors 15 people in her first month, and 15 people in her second month. With this total in her network, she has reached the first management level, and is entitled to good bonuses and commissions on the volume her network achieves.

But what's happened? With 30 people all looking to her to show them what to do next, how much time has she given to each? An hour? An evening? Certainly not more – she's been too busy sponsoring everybody else.

So by the end of the second month, a very large number of the people she sponsored in the first month will have lost interest. They didn't have her ambition and natural sales skills, and because she was the only person they'd met in the business, they didn't know how to go about sponsoring in any other way. So they became despondent, and decided network marketing wasn't for them.

By month three, Salestype 1 was running out of friends to sponsor. Being as good as she was, she still managed to find, let's say, 10. But by now she had lost 15 – and the other 15 weren't doing brilliantly either.

In month four, Salestype 1 looked at her bank account and found her income was declining. Her network simply wasn't performing. Impatient for results, she quit, leaving behind her a lot of disappointed people who would never know what an opportunity they had missed – because they hadn't had the guidance or information necessary to start a business.

Salestype 2

Now the story of *Salestype* 2. He loved the product, and knew exactly how to sell it. In fact, he gave up his existing commission-based sales job to do it. The opportunity seemed so much greater.

In a way, he was right. In the first month he made himself £1,500 clear profit. In month two, with bonuses and commissions paid by the company, he had nearly doubled that. By month three, working all the hours he could, he had pushed his profit above £3,000.

But what happened then? His earnings hit a barrier. He couldn't work any more hours. He couldn't squeeze out any more profit. He was making a decent living – but he was doing it all on his own, behaving as if networking was just direct selling under another name.

So he decided to set aside some time to build a network. And what happened? His retail income immediately dropped. He had left his regular job. His monthly earnings were on a roller-coaster – downwards. Providing he could tough it out for a few lean months, the chances were that he would win through in the end. But he had wasted half a year believing his sales skills alone would make him wealthy.

The teacher-type

And lastly the story of the *Teacher* (not specifically a teacher by profession: just a person able to talk, train, and motivate). She played it by the rules: some retailing, some networking.

Being sensible, she kept her regular job for the time being. She spent 4–6 hours a week retailing, and another 6–8 hours contacting friends, and advising them how best to go about building their own businesses.

The retailing brought in £500–£1,000 a month. The network delivered nothing to begin with, but more and more as time went on. After a few months, income from the two activities added up to more than she was regularly earning. What should she do? Pack in her job and

UNEQUAL OPPORTUNITY?

Zoe Kent, who has built a highly successful business from Nantwich in Cheshire, has found that women who go into network marketing tend to have a different approach from men.

A lot of us are more cautious, particularly at the beginning. We take a while to be convinced that we can do it at all, because we hate the idea of so-called selling to friends. Then, when we realise this isn't what networking is all about, we want to make absolutely sure we're doing it the right way. We spend a long time learning.

The reason, she thinks, is that society as a whole is still male-oriented, so that when women offer men a serious business opportunity, they often feel they have a credibility gap to overcome.

The result in the end is highly beneficial. In the company I work with, nearly half the top earners are women, even though three-quarters of those who join the business in the first place are men.

I have worked out three reasons for this. The first, of course, is that we're teachable – we're prepared to spend time learning. The second is that, by nature, we tend to be more patient, and nurture those we sponsor.

Thirdly, any of us who have brought up children know how to divide our time – we can do a bit of this and a bit of that. We are able to focus intensely on network marketing in the hours we have to spare.

take up network marketing full-time? Carry on with the job but with a handsome part-time income? It was an enviable choice.

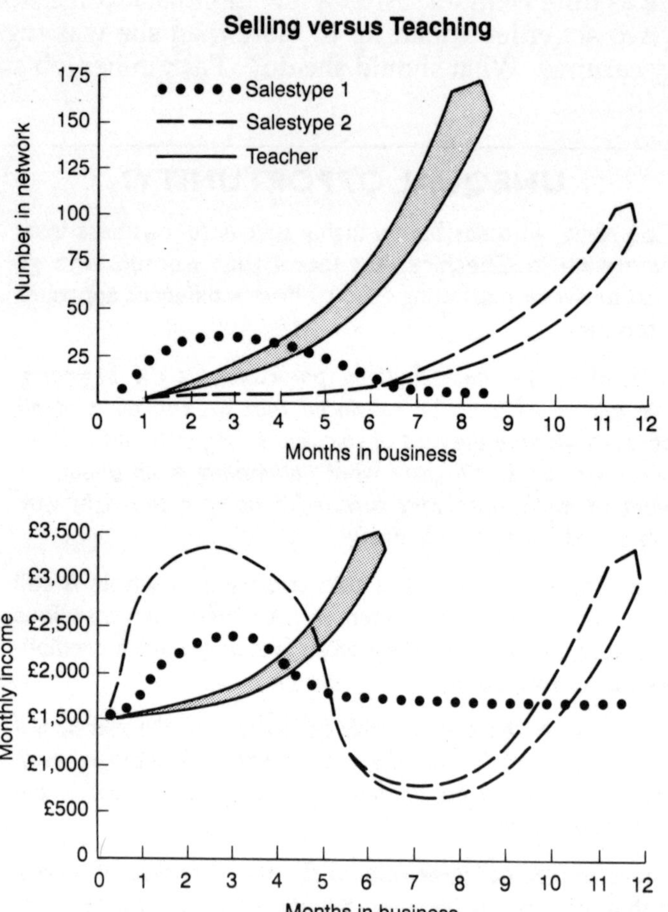

Small wonder that Gary Chamberlain, one of the UK's highest earners in network marketing, has often said: *Offer my network a salesperson or a teacher and I know who I would choose, every time: the teacher.*

Chapter 5

Building and teaching

So much for the theory and the history. Now for the fun.

Network marketing is extremely sociable. It is all about a lot of people doing a little each. Right now, if you've just been introduced to the concept, and shown the product for the first time, it is almost beyond imagination that in a year's time a hundred, two hundred, perhaps even a thousand people could all be earning themselves money and changing their lives – just because of what you do in the next month.

But that's the way it goes.

All you need do is get started – the right way.

You saw the essentials in the last chapter. The fun comes when you start ringing people up, meeting them, sharing the product and the opportunity – and discovering that some of them become even keener than you.

But who will these people be? How can you possibly build a network of this size when, offhand, you can only think of a handful of people you can go to immediately?

The answer is that you only *need* a handful of people. Any more is too much, at least to begin with.

Three is ideal; five is the maximum. That's logical. No successful company executive, or officer in the armed forces, ever has more than five key people he is directly supervising – and often it is as few as three. Similarly in network marketing: you must use your time initially to teach just a handful of people to be as successful as you.

Now if you think back to the experience of California Vitamins, you will remember that 1 × 3 × 3 × 3 × 3 will give you a network of 121, and 1 × 5 × 5 × 5 × 5 will give 781. Anywhere in this range is enough to give you a handsome income from the percentage which the company will pay you on your group's turnover.

So all you need do, right away, is to introduce your first three, four, or five. Who do you ring up, and what do you say?

Your sponsor will encourage you to make a large list of everyone you know (statistically, all adults know several hundred people, if only they could remember their names). Next, you will narrow down your list to the 15 or 20 you would most like to work with – and who are also, in the sponsor's experience, the sort of people most likely to want to succeed in network marketing.

K.I.S.S.

Let's say your first prospect is Jane. You pick up the phone, have a brief hello-and-how-are-you chat with her, and follow it with a short, attention-grabbing invitation. For instance:

Jane, I'm starting a new business, and I'm really excited about it. I'd like your opinion.
You might be able to help me. Join in, even.
Can I come round and talk?

That's all, believe it or not. The right way of getting started is truly that simple. If Jane says yes, make the earliest possible date – that day, if you like – to go with your sponsor and see her so that, with someone experienced beside you, you can show a video, and share the product and the opportunity. Or you might arrange to pick Jane up and take her to a company briefing.

If you make it more complicated and long-winded, and start giving Jane all sorts of details over the phone, the chances are she'll get the wrong picture. It's impossible to tell the whole story on the phone – so it's best to say as little as possible.

AN INVITING PHRASE

David and Lynn Selwood are a husband-and-wife team in network marketing who, from a standing start in June 1990, now have a group of nearly 2,000 independent distributors.

The most rewarding thing – and the most enjoyable – is seeing your family and friends succeed. Our daughter is studying to be a barrister, but is also building a network part-time. When she qualifies to practise, she will be earning enough from network marketing to have the choice of going into law as a career, or working for herself in her own business.

Network marketing is simple, but hard work. When we introduce someone, we give them an hour of our time for an hour of theirs until we are sure our effort is being duplicated.

The thing people find most difficult, to begin with, is to pick up the telephone. They're worried about the reaction the other end. So we have an all-purpose phrase we teach new people to use:

LOOK – THIS IS A BUSINESS CALL. HAVE YOU GOT TIME TO MAKE MONEY TO RUN ALONGSIDE WHAT YOU'RE DOING ALREADY?

Just get a yes or no. Nothing more. Then fix a meeting so that you can explain the opportunity properly.

Remember your own reservations when you first heard of network marketing. Didn't you immediately think of pyramid scams, until the difference was explained to you face to face, rather than over the phone? Wasn't one of your first thoughts: *Honestly, I'm not the right person, I wouldn't want to sell to my friends?*

So "KISS" – keep it short and simple. Be exciting for 30 seconds and that's enough. You're only looking for three, four, or five people. You may well have to ring up three times that number to find them – but like everything else in network marketing, the numbers game works in the end.

Creating a network

Let's say – conservatively – that you arrange meetings with 10 people in your first two or three weeks. All you do, with your sponsor, is show and explain. You need never pressure any of your friends to buy or to join.

At each meeting, you will get one of three responses:

1. *It's not for me – but why not try my friends Mary and Jack? They may be interested.*
2. *The product looks good – I'll try it.*
3. *Being a distributor sounds interesting – tell me more.*

Typically, you might get five Response 1's, two Response 2's, and three Response 3's.

So without trying at all hard, and without "selling", you will have done what both you and the company wants: moved its product to some new end-users, and started a new network.

(Responses 2 and 3 both mean sales, because a new distributor will need some product to start doing business).

From just 10 meetings you have set up, your network will begin to form something like this:

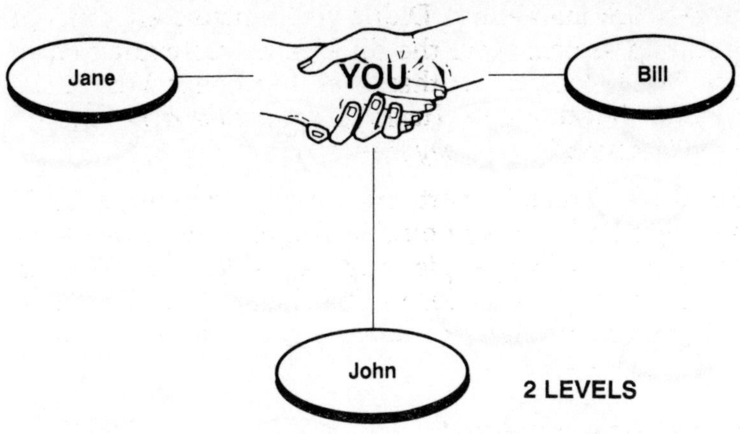

To go on to the next level in your network, you contact more people. This time, you probably won't know them. The seven friends you saw in stage one who weren't interested, or bought the product, will have given you some names of their own friends who might want to be offered the opportunity as well.

For the time being, you are looking for only two more people to join your network at the 2nd level, to give you your handful of five.

Because additionally, you now have three new distributors in your network who are going to do exactly the same as you: meet 10 people. You will be spending time showing them how to do it – teaching them, just as your sponsor helped you with your first calls, and going along with them.

If they get more or less the same results as you – which they should do if you have sponsored people as keen as you are – they too will sponsor two or three people each, and make a few retail sales.

Your network will begin to look something like this:

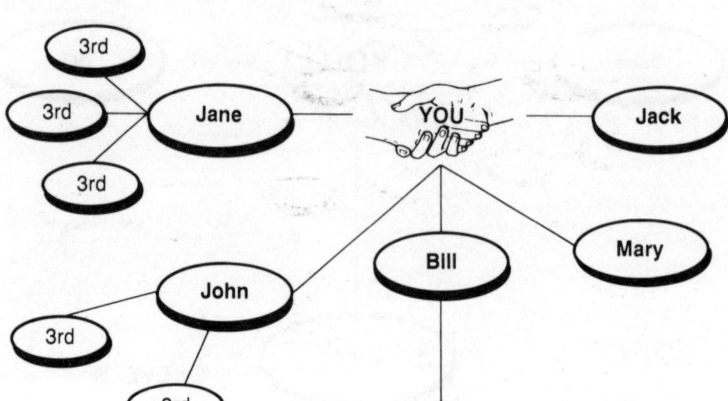

By now, at the end of, say, the second month, you have a full hand. Mary and Jack both joined, so you have enough 2nd level people, and for the moment, you do not want to create any more legs. Your time will be spent mostly on teaching others to do the same as you, with some retailing on the side.

Now you want to create depth in your network, so that it has stability, and allow you to profit through many generations downline from you. With 11 people, you will have made a good start. The network will already have a life of its own. What shape it takes will depend on the quality of the 5 people you have put in the front-line, and on the teaching example you are able to set. You must train, encourage, and motivate. Phone every-one in your group. Go with them to their new people. Take them to training sessions, and let them learn.

Two things are sure:

1. Your network won't develop evenly and regularly as per the 5 times mathematical model.
2. At the same time the power of numbers will win out in the end.

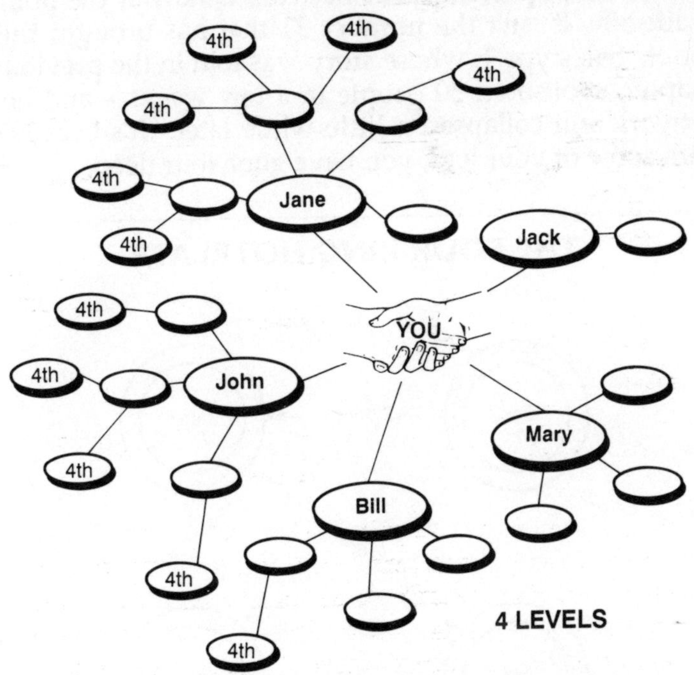

Typically, after a few weeks or a few months, you could have a network that looks something like this. Notice how unevenly it has developed. Jane is leading the field, with a network of 11, plus herself. John has six, Bill five, Mary three, and Jack one.

This is the way it usually happens. You will find that one of your legs develops startlingly fast. Another may never get off the ground. In another, an unexpected star performer may emerge – someone who is going to earn even more money than you. (Cross your fingers that this will happen: a handful of people like that, and you will be very wealthy).

But the 31 you now have in your network is a large enough number, with most companies, to put you in line for substantial bonuses, and the first position of management.

Even more important, your network is now at the point of lift-off. It isn't the number 31 that has brought this about. Salestype 1, whose story was told in the previous chapter, sponsored 30 people in a few weeks – and her network still collapsed a little while later. It's because, with some of your legs, you have gone four deep.

THE FOUR-RING HOTPLATE

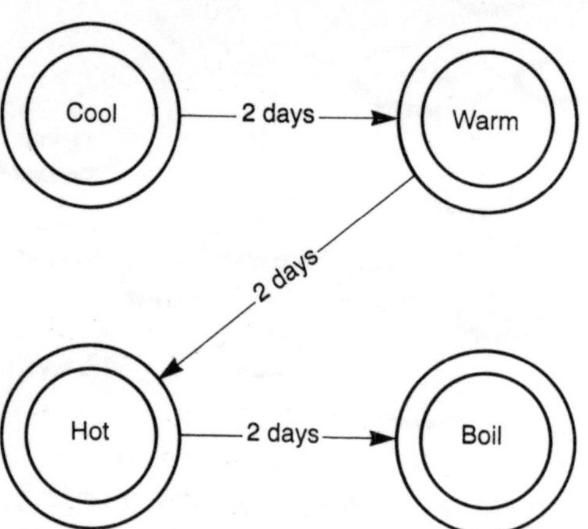

One almost sure way of blowing out a good prospect is to try to explain everything at once. It has the same effect as putting a glass of cold water directly on to the boiling plate of a cooker.

Take it gently, but keep the momentum going. "Cool" is the first short telephone call. "Warm" is a visit lasting half an hour or so while you watch a video and show the product. "Hot" is when you introduce them to other people doing well in the business, for instance at a company briefing. "Boiling" is when you have a session setting goals, and make the initial product order.

Let your prospect read this book anywhere between cool and boiling.

Four deep

This is perhaps the most important practical lesson you will have to learn if you are to be successful in network marketing.

Until you have built a leg four deep, it isn't truly self-replicating.

Let's think about the first person you sponsored: Jane. By bringing her into the business, it looks at first glance as though you have duplicated yourself -

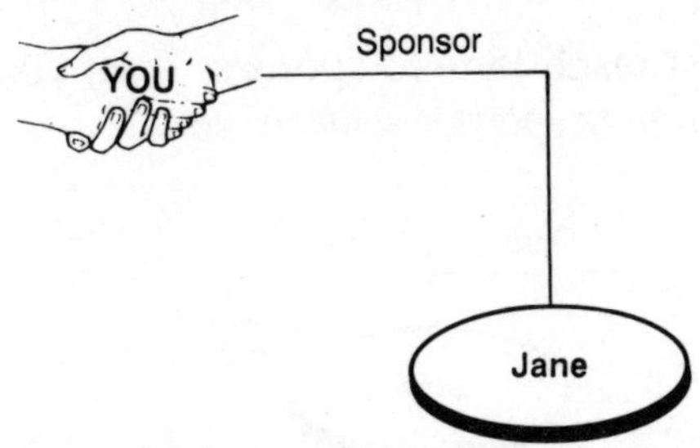

But you haven't – because Jane knows almost nothing yet about practicalities and techniques of building a business of her own. So you go one stage better: you teach Jane that to have her own network, she needs to sponsor people herself. Jane promptly rings up her close friend Tom, who thinks it's a great idea, and signs a registration form.

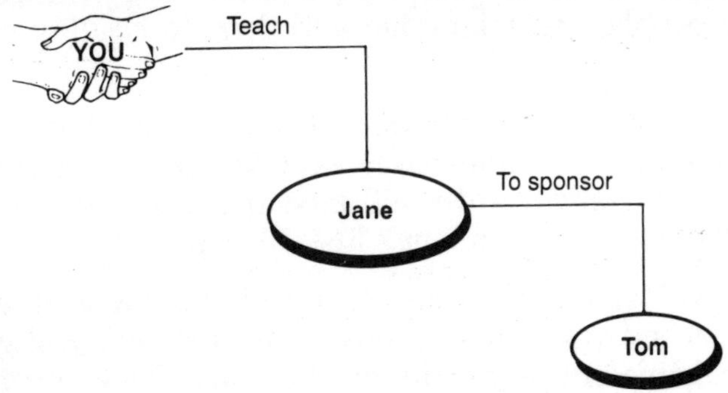

Deceptively, this looks better, as though you and Jane are now on your way. But it is still not self-perpetuating. Because the only thing Tom knows about the business is what Jane showed him – that he has to sponsor other close friends. Let's say he makes a few unsatisfactory phone calls and gets no results. What happens? He gives up. Your line stops right there. Then Jane, too, becomes disheartened. Now your leg is producing no results at all.

To prevent this happening, you have to teach the *right teaching attitudes at the very beginning.*

You don't just teach Jane to sponsor Tom, you teach Jane *how to teach Tom to sponsor someone else.*

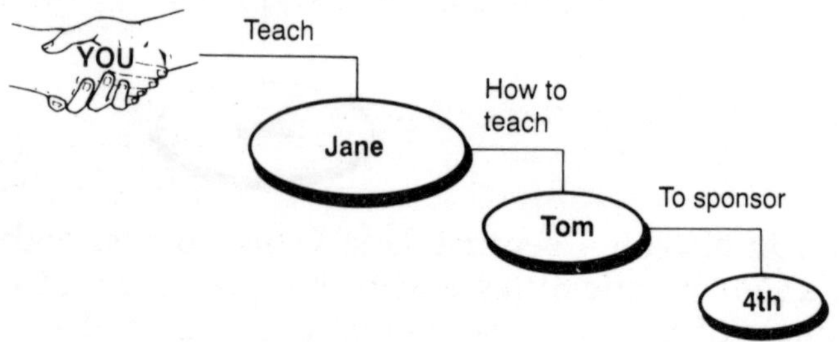

This is where the effort and skills in network building take place: at the very beginning. You will be patiently spending time with Jane, establishing her goals, working through her list of prospects, phoning and visiting her new people, and taking her and them to training meetings.

Jane will copy what you do – be sure of that. She'll have the reassurance of someone experienced by her side in the early stages, and she'll pass this habit on. It will duplicate itself down Jane's line, 10 or 15 deep.

You will have put yourself in a position where, at levels far beyond your direct control, your network will grow and thrive entirely of its own accord. Once you have done this you are secure. You can go away on holiday –

or better still, go and create another leg – safe in the knowledge that this part of your network now has a built-in dynamic for growth.

Network growth

How far and how fast your network grows will depend on:

a) How soon you find three, four, or five good people. It can take days – or months. You may well have to contact several times the eventual number. But they're around. You just have to keep at it.

b) How many hours a week you're prepared to spend teaching them, and going to meetings with them – and doing the same with the first new level of people they introduce.

After a solid year in the business – *providing you remember to teach* how to teach – you will probably find 100 – 600 in your network. Those who consistently teach the right habits can always reach the 100 plus level – and from then on, the sky is the limit.

Whatever the figure, your network will grow so long as you remember to build four deep:

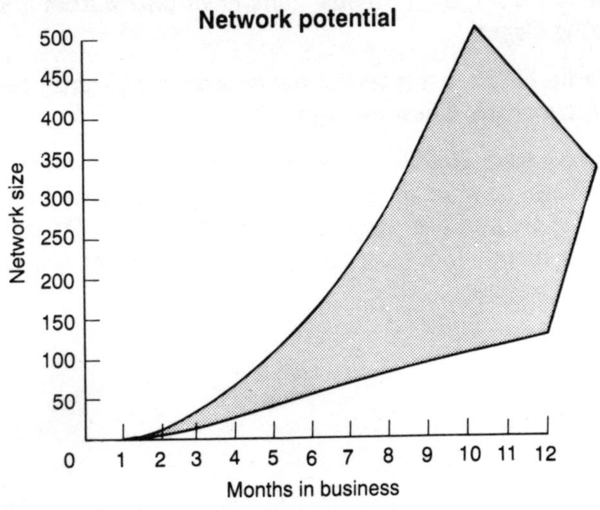

SATURATION

If you take geometric progression to its logical conclusion, it raises a question which deserves answering:

Network marketing is obviously booming – so what's going to happen when it saturates? Surely everyone will be in on it soon, and there'll be nowhere for me to go?

The general point of comfort here is that although, numerically, if you multiply 5 × 5 a few times (11 times, in fact), you run out of adult population in the UK, the reality is that human nature stops it happening. Most people are fundamentally too idle to benefit from network marketing, except by buying product.

In the UK at the end of 1991, perhaps 500,000 out of an adult population of about 40 million were to some degree active in the networking business: hardly more than 1%. In the US, the proportion was about double that. Even when the UK reaches US levels, there will still be 39 million people who remain as potential distributors, or buyers.

Moreover, there is not a network marketing company in the UK which is sponsoring distributors at anything like the net rate of population growth – so however fast anyone sponsors, the potential number of distributors is still getting bigger.

Charlie Elliott, a successful distributor in the small town of Altrincham, Cheshire, says:

We only have 20,000 houses in our area. Just in these surroundings, no more than eight minutes drive from my home, I have sponsored five people who are all earning £50,000 a year or more. That's just the beginning. Saturation is a practical impossibility.

Chapter 6

Is it for you?

Dream for a few moments.

Imagine Jane, after two or three years in the business.

She is getting ready to travel on the journey of a lifetime. She's in her bedroom, putting the last few things in her suitcases. All her bills have been paid – she's going away with a carefree mind. A taxi will soon be at the door to take her to the airport, where a porter will look after her luggage and show her to the lounge for travellers flying first class. Then she's going to take off for a paradise island, and stay there as long as she likes to eat wonderful food, swim in a warm sea, and soak up the sun.

An enticing dream? Too fanciful? Not at all.

In network marketing, you are encouraged to dream your wildest dreams, and turn these into goals that you picture in your mind. Then you draw up a realistic action plan so that you can attain them within a timescale which you set yourself.

Jane's dream was: *I want to be free to do what I want to do, when I want to do it.*

To make this tangible, she visualized her first goal: *I want to go on the most luxurious holiday money can buy, without worrying about whether I can afford it.*

And to make this achievable, she wrote down a series of mini goals and deadlines, so that she had something to aim for on the way, and knew how many hours she would have to work to make them happen.

In broad outline, the goals were simple. Within six months, she would have at least 30 people in her network; within a year, 100; within 18 months, 300; within two years, 1,000. These were promises to herself, and she wouldn't break them, no matter what. She wrote down in detail her plan of how many people she would need to contact, week by week and day by day.

Then, in the third year, automatically, she would have enough money for her holiday.

There is a strangely under-publicised branch of science (see Box below) which shows that the human mind has an extraordinary capacity, working well below the level of consciousness, to direct us to our goals – providing our desire to achieve these goals is strong enough, and

CYBERNETICS

In the 1940s, scientists working at the Massachusetts Institute of Technology coined a new word, *cybernetics*, to describe the work they were doing on sophisticated, self-correcting guidance systems for missiles. The word comes from the Greek for "helmsman".

All animals – humans particularly – are biological cybernetic systems, far more advanced than any computer system yet developed. Throughout their lives, they are capable of learning from mistakes, and use a natural process of feedback to steer them to their target – like a baby determined to learn to walk.

But they can only do this if they know precisely what the target, or "goal", is. Ill-defined goals bring erratic helmsmanship. By contrast, the human mind will chart its way infallibly to a goal which is clear and focussed, taking the best route possible in changing circumstances.

we keep reminding ourselves what they are. Academic research has shown that 95% of people never set goals for themselves. The 5% who do – and better still, those who write down their goals and refer to them daily – achieve results far and away better than the rest.

Of course, a luxury holiday may not be your over-riding ambition. What might it be? To stop working? Buy a better house? Move to a another area? Spend more time with your family? Do something about the way your parents live? Put your children in a good school?

Whatever your personal desire, one of the first things you will be taught when you come into the business is: *write down your goals.* Colin Turner, one of the best trainers in network marketing, says emphatically:

GOALS ARE AS ESSENTIAL TO SUCCESS AS AIR IS TO LIFE.

Changing from within

The second thing you will be taught also has a psychological basis. It sounds easy, but is tough when you come to do it: *Be prepared to change.*

Jane, when she decided she was going to have a paradise holiday, had to change. Deep down inside, she made up her mind that, more than anything else in the world, she wanted to get out of her rut and make this journey. Instead of watching TV, she spent her evenings and weekends on the phone, or visiting people, or going to meetings.

And because she was so determined, and was contacting and teaching so many new people, quite quickly she found herself growing in self-belief. The more dedicated she was, the more confident she became. And finally she found herself packing her bags and waiting for the taxi to arrive.

Shay O'Brien tells new people coming into the business:

If you want your life to change – your financial status, your enjoyment, your confidence – you yourself have to change. You have to get out of your comfort zone and behave more positively than you ever have before. The money in network marketing is incidental. What you've jumped on to is a vehicle for transforming your life.

Most people make the mistake, initially, of underestimating the power of network marketing. Understandably, they lack belief – until they have been to enough meetings, and had the chance of talking to people who have revolutionised the way they live.

But the fact is that network marketing is an extremely sophisticated distribution system which swiftly and effectively moves product from factory to end-user. Because it is so simple in concept, so easy for people to join, and so flexible in the way it provides additional income, nobody can be blamed for first thinking, this seems too good to be true.

The alternatives

But what are the alternatives, if you want to earn some extra money, or start a business of your own? Compare it with any other type of commercial opportunity currently being advertised. Most of these involve telephone selling, or badly-paid hourly rates for repetitive work – which in any event would mean working for somebody else, rather than yourself.

As another way of making money from home, you could market whatever skills you happen to have – gardening, or sewing, or decorating, or cooking, or cleaning, or B & B, or consultancy. Here two problems crop up: you have to find a way of letting people know you are available (advertising, mail-shots, etc.); and you are limited by the fact that there are only 24 hours in a day, of which you have to sleep for at least six. And how much an hour can you charge? £10? £20? The retail prospects, alone, from network marketing are probably better.

Otherwise, there is virtually no business which you can start up without capital. Franchises for good products in good areas offer a reasonable prospect – but the costs will be in excess of £25,000. Even if you are successful, you will be tied down to long regular hours, overheads, and the headaches which go with hiring staff, none of which apply to network marketing.

Why it's so simple

By contrast, it is the low-risk, low-overhead, elements of networking, together with the way in which it is in everyone else's interest for you to succeed, which appeals to most people when they have looked at it carefully.

The networking company itself, if it is a good one, will handle most of the elements which make start-up businesses vulnerable, including:

* Product development
* Financing costs of manufacture and stock
* Administration costs of supplying distributors
* Costs of administering network payroll
* Handling of regulatory bodies

For your part, you simply make a small initial investment in "tools of the trade" – stock, sales aids, training meetings. You will incur certain running costs: probably an increased phone bill, and some additional petrol.

But that's about it. If you change your mind about the product or the company after, say, a month, and just pack the whole thing in, you will have wasted a bit of time, and perhaps £50 to £100 on sales aids, petrol, and the 10% which isn't refunded on your 90% buy-back guarantee.

Part-time or full-time

You don't need to go full-time to succeed. Although you should regard network marketing as a start-up business (even if you are doing it only a few hours a week to begin with), the vast majority of people in network marketing start part-time and remain part-time. They're happy with the extra income: in round figures, anything from £250 to £1,500 a month. That in itself is enough to change their lifestyle.

You need only go full-time if you want to build a serious business, and the thought of £30,000 to £300,000 a year or more excites you.

The sheer range of people making money out of network marketing shows that you don't need special skills. There are ex-bricklayers driving new Jaguars, and plenty of parents putting their children through expensive schools. Background, education, age, sex, colour – it simply doesn't matter who you are and where you come from.

A puzzled City businessman took a look at the success stories and said:

I don't understand it – all the wrong sort of people seem to be making money.

The most important skills to develop – and we all have them in us – are being able to talk to people, to explain, and to motivate. Since, to begin with, you will be doing this just to friends and colleagues, it's easily within your grasp.

Commitment

If network marketing (even part-time) means setting up a business, then it carries along with it some of the penalties of being your own boss. The hours can be somewhat unsocial – if you have a full-time day job, you will have to give up a bit of TV in the evenings, and some of your recreation at weekends.

And like any business, network marketing will take time to deliver. Although you can make decent extra money from the day you receive your first delivery of product, it could be six months to a year before your network is substantial.

In fact, a year's commitment to the business is the period you should have in mind. Anything shorter than 12 months is not enough to even out the ups and downs that the whims of human nature will bring to your network.

Given this length of time, the sheer power of geometric progression will win through. Most people quit network marketing in the first few months, when things seem to be going too slowly. So long as you keep on sponsoring and retailing, networking is as simple as a two (or five) times table. The only thing is: simple doesn't mean easy.

But consider the alternatives again. What other system offers you such low-risk earnings as you go along, and a pot of gold if you are successful? What other scheme offers the possibility of complete financial independence in 3 – 5 years' time with virtually no capital investment up front? Indeed, ask any other start-up businessperson if he or she expects to be financially secure at the end of 12 months, and what would the answer be: are you joking?

The basic concept of network marketing is so sound that it deserves to be repeated:

YOU CAN MAKE A LIVING MARKETING A PRODUCT. BUT YOU CAN MAKE A FORTUNE BY BUILDING A NETWORK AND TEACHING OTHERS TO DO THE SAME.

Everybody helps

At this point, there is a question almost everyone asks:

Network marketing seems brilliant for those who got in early – but what about us late starters?

In other words, are you too late to make a fortune? There is a comforting answer: no, you're not.

Network marketing is played on a level playing field. If you complete enough circuits of the running track, you will catch up or overtake those who started before you, but are now easing up because their business has gone so well.

And it is much more like recreational jogging than competitive racing. Perhaps the strangest thing that newcomers to network marketing find, coming as they often do straight from the dog-eat-dog world of commercial business, is that everyone wishes you well, and encourages you to succeed.

Partly this is because the field is wide open. Because saturation, in practice, can never remotely happen, there is simply no need to compete. But more than that, *the system rewards the basic human urge to help others. When you do, you prosper.*

There is an American description of this:

You can have anything in the world that you want, simply by helping enough other people to get what they want.

The founders of network marketing may not have realized at the time what they were doing, but they wedded two of the most powerful forces in the human psyche. We like to get, and we like to give. It's a happy and unusual marriage.

The result, most people discover when they join network marketing, is a camaraderie unlike any other form of business. At meetings, you come face to face with dozens of successful people all urging you to be equally successful. Your network takes on a life of its own. It can be drawn as a family tree – and in a sense it becomes one, with everyone looking to you as its founder.

So how do you decide where to begin?

Chapter 7

Choosing a company

You may be half-way there already. A friend has rung you up, shown you a video, introduced you to networking, and suggested this book. Right?

Well, if you know someone who is already making money out of the business, that's a good starting point. You'll be able to get first hand answers to your questions.

Because if you're like most people, you will see the potential right away, and will be attracted by the idea of making some extra money. But you'll want to take a hard look at whether this particular opportunity is the right one for you.

There are just two basic questions:

* *Is the company a good one?*
* *Do you like the products?*

The company

Think very carefully about the company. What you should be looking for is one whose track record shows that it will still be around in five to 10 years' time. That is to say, it will have experienced and high-quality management, a history of growth without financial upheavals, and a commitment to updating its product range.

On the other side of the coin, any prudent business adviser would advise extreme caution about becoming involved with a company that may seem to be growing very rapidly, but does not yet have least two years' trading figures to support this.

So here is a checklist you can use:

Stability and trading record. Has it been running successfully for a while, or is it a new venture? If the former, is it still growing? If the latter, is it financially well backed? Does it belong to the Direct Selling Association?

Manufacturing capability. Does it manufacture its own products? If not, be cautious – reliance on outside suppliers creates greater risk.

Marketing Plan. Does it give you the opportunity of making money at many levels? Is there any limit on your network size, and how much money you can make? Is the business concept simple (even if the Marketing Plan is complex)? Is your profit margin generous?

Promises. Does it hold out the prospect of you making a lot of money quickly? – say, more than £5,000 a month in the first few months. If so, be wary, even though it's possible.

Training. How good are the sales aids? Were you impressed by the video? Is your sponsor keen to help you – and teach you how to teach others? Is there training put on for your group by distributors and the company?

Risk. How much do you need to spend to get started?

Attitude. This is very subjective. Keep your eyes and ears open at meetings. Does it feel professional? Do people look successful? Do you get the impression they are enjoying themselves – is there that sense of camaraderie which is so essential to good network marketing? Are a lot of new people like yourself taking an interest? (A good sign – it means the company is thriving. Never worry about saturation.)

The Product

When you've examined the company, think about the product. Here again there is a businesslike checklist you can go through.

Mass market. Is it something everyone could use – and want? Does it have universal appeal? If it doesn't, how big is its market? What proportion of your immediate friends would enjoy using it?

Market advantage. Does it have something genuinely new to offer? Does the product have something special? What is the competition? If it's so new it has no track record, are you confident it will find a marketplace? Is it company policy to introduce additional new lines so that you will have something else to offer your network in the future?

Reliability. Is it reliable and simple, or hi-tech and complex? You don't want to find yourself with warranty problems, or or needing to go back to people's homes to fix or replace what they have bought.

Demonstrability. Can you readily show people its benefits, by demonstrating it in their home? Can they borrow it and try it out? Or are they buying it on your say-so alone? – in which case you may need to develop sales skills.

Pricing. Is it priced to sell? Is it good value? Will people think it a rip-off? What is its price compared with the competition?

Repeat sales. Is it consumable? That is to say, will the buyer come back automatically for more, if satisfied? Without this, you will constantly have to find new customers.

Finally, and most subjectively of all:

WOULD YOU BUY IT YOURSELF?

This is the crucial, bottom-line question. However good the company, and the business opportunity, you have to sense the need for the product. It is a gut reaction. You must be able to say to yourself: *Yes – I'd be happy talking to friends about this.*

That's not to say that right now, at this very moment, you have to have absolute belief. It would hardly be credible if you did. You need time to evaluate both the product and the marketing plan.

But you should feel instinctively that:

a) *You would like to try the product yourself*

b) *The timing in the marketplace seems good*

c) *Some of your friends might like it to try it too*

If you're positive about all three, everything else will fall into place.

Your choice

So what's on offer? What will you feel most comfortable talking about? Something that is really good value? Something which is environmentally friendly? Household consumables? The need for clean air and water? Jewellery? Perfume? Diet and health aids? Security systems?

There's a large choice nowadays. An Appendix at the end of the book gives brief profiles of the major players on the field, together with one or two smaller ones for comparison. They vary a lot in financial strength. Think about this if you decide to shop around. Think about their recent track record in growth, too. It is a strong indicator of how successful you yourself might be, working within their system.

As to how much money you can expect to make out of working with a particular company, you will discover a common pattern. Successful part-timers are making £500 – £1,500 a month, and sometimes a good deal more.

For those looking to create a serious business, the questionnaire uncovered one person in the UK who made more than £1m in 1991. Many were in the £100,000 – £500,000+ a year bracket.

When you choose which product line you might like, one aspect you should think of is its price to the end-user. In network marketing, products are divided into what are known as "low-ticket" and "high-ticket" items.

With the first, you have to share a lot of product for a little profit on each. With the second, it is the reverse: just one or two sales a week of a product retailing at £150 – £200 will give you a reasonable start-up income.

National Safety Associates

One company which can undoubtedly offer financial strength, exceptional recent growth, and known product demand, is National Safety Associates – NSA for short. It falls into the "high-ticket" category, although with a product range priced from £40 to £400, "medium-ticket" might be a fairer description.

For those still nervous about the "selling" aspect of network marketing, one major plus is that the company insists you do not have to sell in the traditional sense. Instead, you loan out product for a week on a "Try it, you'll like it" basis.

As David Hunt, one of their National Marketing Directors, has put it:

> *5% of people have sales skills, 95% don't. With NSA's approach, you can turn the figures the other way around. 95% of people find it absolutely natural to lend something they themselves enjoy. Why not? Lending and sharing are part of normal life.*

The success of this system is one reason why NSA, in each year from 1989 to 1991, appeared in Inc. Magazine's list of 500 fastest growing private companies in the US – and in '90 and '91, in the top 25. In 1991, they were also the 4th fastest growing of all foreign-owned companies in the UK.

The history of fast-growing private companies shows that this rate of growth doesn't go on for ever. From now on, there are bound to be periods of consolidation. But it is still an outstanding recent performance – and you have to ask: what, besides their sales method, do they have going for them?

* * *

First, a subjective note. NSA believes that, compared with other networking companies, it has a higher proportion of seriously interested new people from the professions and from the business world. After visiting a large number of NSA's meetings, this seems to be true.

Of course, at the biggest meetings, where there were 2,000 or 3,000 people, I found the cross-section of the population described at the beginning of this book – people of all ages and types, the ones who prompted a City businessman to complain that the "wrong" sort of people seem to be making money in network marketing – that *anyone can learn to do it.*

But additionally, as I interviewed and researched the subject, I found that at NSA's meetings in particular, I lost count of the number of businesspeople, experts in financial services, accountants, and even bankers, who told me that they would never see an opportunity like it in their lifetime, and that they were now committed.

I came, after a while, to agree with them. While there are undoubted opportunities with other network marketing companies (and equally, some you should be guarded about), NSA seems to me currently to have a unique combination of advantages, and I am going to spend the remainder of this book describing why others besides myself came to this conclusion.

What is it that convinced them? What is making all these successful people sell their businesses and give up their jobs to join in with NSA and start working for themselves?

Their bottom line is this: they have decided in their own minds that:

a) Network marketing is the growth business of the decade – like a franchise without the initial outlay.

b) NSA is a well-run company with a sound financial base and an excellent management track record.

c) NSA has put in place a product range which is universal in appeal, and is priced to sell.

d) NSA's growth record over the last five years shows that it has an exceptional marketing strategy.

The environmental market

The market factor which lies behind NSA's success is a simple one:

WE ALL DRINK WATER, AND WE ALL BREATHE AIR.

BUT NOWADAYS, WE WORRY ABOUT IT.

This is a hot market. Not a day goes by without media coverage about how our surroundings are being damaged and polluted. The UK persistently delays the targeted date by which it will meet EC municipally-treated water standards. A 1989 Department of Environment survey showed that more than 70% of people were concerned about the quality of drinking water, compared with 5% ten years previously.

When it comes to the air we breathe, the dangers of passive smoking are now well documented. Indoor air, where we spend 95% of our time, is up to 20 times more polluted than outdoors. Air conditioning systems, particularly old ones, simply re-circulate contaminated air.

The "sick building syndrome" is now an established health hazard.

Public reaction to this in the marketplace can best be seen in the explosive growth in sales of bottled water. Ten years ago, they were less than 200,000 litres a week. Today they are 10 million litres a week, and are expected to double by 1996. An article in Life magazine said that *by the year 2000 nobody will be drinking tap water.*

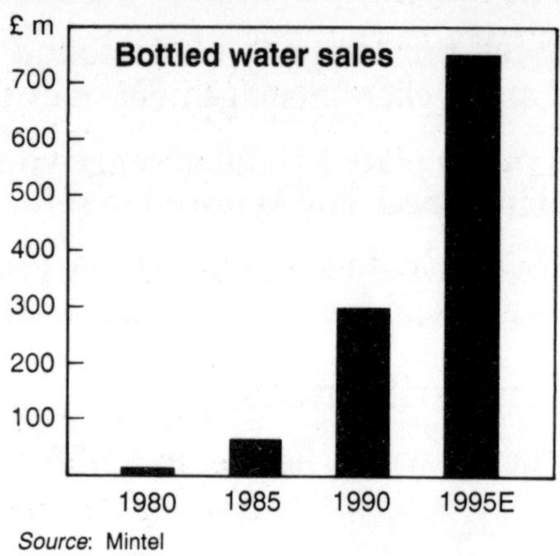

Source: Mintel

This growth has been achieved in spite of the fact that carrying bottled water back home from the supermarket is inconvenient and (at 35p to more than 60p per litre) expensive. Many bottled waters cost more to buy than petrol. Its safety is also unreliable. A number of reports have condemned bottled water suppliers for producing sub-standard quality.

Back at the beginning of the bottled water boom, there was an obvious market opportunity for any company astute enough to spot it. The company needed only to be able to say:

Don't bother going shopping. We can clean up your water at home, fresh out of your taps, for much less money.

This simple but perceptive piece of foresight was what launched NSA to its present heights.

The company

NSA was incorporated in Memphis in 1970 by Jay Martin. He has been president ever since, and has had the same top management team since 1975. During NSA's first decade of corporate life, it became the leading direct sales company in the US for fire extinguishers and smoke alarms, achieving a total of $100m in sales.

Then Jay Martin looked at industries and new markets which were likely to continue to grow to the year 2000 and beyond. He settled for products that would let people take action themselves, in their homes, to make their lives more comfortable in an increasingly polluted environment.

He has explained how he arrived at his company's new philosophy:

When I looked at where industry had been focussed, decade by decade, I saw that in the '50s it had been on plastics, in the '60s on the space program, the '70s on energy conservation, and the '80s on computer technology.

There was no question in my mind that the number one concern in the '90s, and for many years after, would be the environment.

NSA's first policy decision was to manufacture a water filtration unit that could easily be fitted in the home, and then forgotten about. There must be no maintenance hassle, and no need to change filters. The unit also had to be highly cost-effective, compared with bottled water, over its 3-year life.

The product NSA came up with was named the 100S. To begin with, NSA used the same direct sales force as had been successfully selling fire extinguishers. Sales were modest – less than $2m a year.

Then the company moved into network marketing. Sales immediately began to increase.

Finally it introduced the concept of a trial period for the product, with a demonstration counter-top model. Distributors were encouraged to say simply: *Try it, you'll like it* – and go back a week later for the customer's reaction.

As a marketing formula it worked at once. And it led to lift-off.

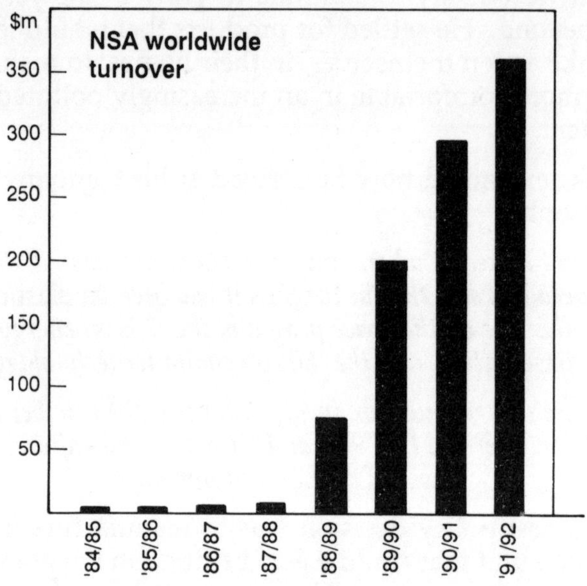

This extraordinary growth – 4,000% in the last five years – has been achieved partly through expansion to other territories. In 1988/89 NSA moved into Canada and the UK, then Eire, and in 1991 Germany. Wherever it has gone, it has dominated the market. In the US, its water filtration systems outsell all other systems combined (some 40, sold under 400 different brand names). In the UK, it is market leader.

In 1991, NSA International generated more than one-third of total sales. The UK growth chart showed a similar pattern to the US:

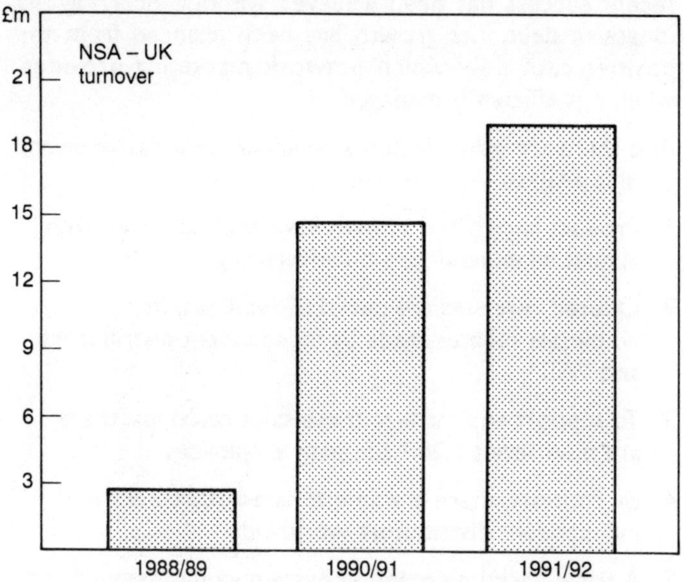

There are plans to open up in other EC countries, and in Australia, during the remainder of the '90s. Here, from day one, distributors will be able to market, as well as water systems, NSA's second range of environmental products, launched in 1989 in the US and in 1991 in the UK: for air filtration. NSA has also told its distributors that major new products will be launched about every 18 months. A pre-school learning system, Wings, is already being marketed successfully in the US.

So when I looked through my company check list, including the crucial one of whether it looked as though the company would still be stable and successful in five to ten years' time, NSA passed comfortably. It was time to look at the product range in more detail.

COMPANY ANALYSIS

One remarkable result of using network marketing as the basis for corporate sales is that NSA's phenomenal recent success has been achieved without incurring any longterm debt. Its growth has been financed from the positive cash flow which network marketing provides, when it is efficiently managed.

And there are other features which are impressive to any outside analyst.

1. Product launch and growth have been achieved with almost nil expenditure on advertising.
2. Quoted revenues are net of all retail profits, wholesale rebates made by independent distributors, and VAT.
3. To support and manage these sales revenues, there are now about 1,200 company employees.
4. By contrast, there are an estimated 50,000 active independent distributors worldwide.
5. A triple back-up computer system, commissioned at a cost of $6 million, provides a monthly printout to each distributor detailing transactions in his or her organisation.
6. The company has its own manufacturing and shipping facility with capacity for expansion to all forecast growth levels.

Joining NSA means getting the backing of a powerful international company – while still having complete control of your own business.

Chapter 8

Tastes good, smells good

Municipal water companies in the UK, newly privatised, face major challenges. They have bought treatment systems delivering water through often old and leaking pipes. At the same time as our climate is becoming drier, the demand for water is increasing both in homes and in industry.

The water we drink amounts to only about 1% of the water we use. The authorities, naturally, are focussed on how to supply and make a profit on the other 99%. Making our water taste good has a fairly low priority. Making it safe, and making it more abundant, are what count.

In spite of media stories about shrimps coming out of the taps, or about chemical contamination incidents causing water to be cut off for a few days, or about failure to meet the demanding EC standards, UK tap water is almost always perfectly safe to drink, even if in some areas it doesn't look or smell good.

The trouble is, the only commercially viable way of removing bacteria from water – that is, of making it safe – is by mixing it with chlorine. And chlorine, whether or not it has long-term effects on your health, tastes and smells foul.

As a water engineer said to me privately: *We won't get sued for putting in extra chlorine, if that's what is needed. But we'll certainly be sued if we don't.*

So this is why some reservoirs, after an emergency, have

had a double or treble fix of chlorine – and you can still taste it. And why you can expect chlorine levels generally to rise as the years go by.

When you drink bottled water carried home from the supermarket, the main reason it tastes better is because it contains little or no chlorine. This has often been removed by passing the water through a bed of granular activated carbon.

NSA's filtration system

With an NSA bottled water unit, you are putting the water through the same process as many of the bottled water manufacturers, but at a fraction of the price.

The chlorinated taste of tapwater, and the inconvenience of bottled water, has led many observers to forecast that during the 1990s, water filters in the kitchen will be as common as microwave ovens:

Sales of home water filtration devices should soon exceed 1 million per year in the UK alone – Financial Times.

Tougher water quality standards will benefit water filter sales – Wall Street Journal.

Water filters will be the next standard kitchen appliance – Woman's Own.

As many as 50% of the UK's 23 million homes may be using water filtration systems by the middle of the decade. NSA's track record suggests that more than half the units will be theirs. The cost to consumers will be in the same sort of bracket as they are accustomed to paying for other household appliances: £40 – £400.

The 100S

By far the most popular of NSA's range is the 100S, a modest-sized cylinder which is easily plumbed in under the kitchen sink, usually with its own special fountain tap. It costs £155 (excluding VAT, tap, and fitting), and is fully warranted to produce good tasting water for three years.

As in the US, convenience is probably its most powerful marketing point. The filters do not have to be changed. There is no need for back-flushing. With no attention, its capacity of 45,000 litres works out at less than 1p per litre.

At the end of the 3-year warranty, NSA writes to the customer asking if they wish for a replacement. There is a high take-up rate. Distributors receive the same commission on repeat orders as on the original sale.

The convenience, plus the "less than 1p a litre" price tag, gives the 100S a distinct market advantage. Distributors can honestly say:

For little over £1 a week, you will have as much clean water as you can possibly want.

The value, compared with other systems producing the same volume of filtered water, is striking.

How the 100S works

Chlorinated tap water flows first of all through a screen mesh that removes undissolved particles. Then, in the body of the filter, tiny activated carbon granules provide a large surface area to absorb the chlorine. The carbon is also impregnated with minute amounts of silver, to prevent bacteria growing within the unit.

After a final multi-micron screening, the water comes out clear, tastes good, and smells good (that is to say, it smells of nothing at all). All the models have been stringently tested and approved by the Environmental Protection Agency in the US, conform to UK British Standards, and have the approval of Lyne, Martin and Radford, the leading public analysts in the UK.

JUG FILTERS:

These need constant attention. They are prone to bacteria growth unless carefully washed and rinsed (and for this reason are banned in Germany). Filters must be changed every week or two weeks.

To the initial cost of £10–£20 must be added filter costs of about £2 per 50–75 litres. The cost for 45,000 litres will exceed £1,000.

FILTRATION UNITS:

These vary greatly in price and quality, from £60 to more than £3,000. Not all have silver to combat bacteria growth. Most have only a 1-year guarantee. Usually, filters must be bought and changed every 3,000–6,000 litres at a cost of £10–£40.

Typically, the 3-year, 45,000-litre cost of a unit equivalent to NSA's, plus filters, would exceed £400 – more than double NSA's price.

The 100S accounts for most of NSA's end-user water filtration sales. There is a range of other water purification systems targeted at specific uses.

Air products

Unlike the water treatment market, where comparisons can be made with the bottled water industry, and where rigorous testing standards apply, the market for air treatment is largely undeveloped.

But just as everyone would like to have clean water, obviously everyone would like clean air. Feedback from sales of the water filtration units convinced NSA that air pollution was as big, or even bigger, an environmental problem. Before developing a product range, NSA looked at existing domestic and office air treatment systems, and found many of them largely ineffective.

Ionisation units, for example, merely send out a negative electrical charge which causes particles to become attracted to positively charged surfaces, such as walls and tables. Typically, a grimy black residue collects around the unit.

Electronic air cleaners are a slight improvement, attracting particles to an electrically charged plate inside the unit. But these decrease rapidly in efficiency, and neither they nor ionisation systems do anything about gases and odours.

NSA decided that the market was for filtration systems which would physically remove microscopic particles of dust and bacteria, and also absorb and neutralize most gases and odours. Rather than develop a system or systems from scratch, NSA hunted down state-of-art scientific technology which could be built into units which they would manufacture themselves.

All the units which were designed, and are now being sold, contain a series of hi-tech filters which do precisely this. Their price range is £93.50 to £359.00, plus VAT.

The air market

Air unit sales already account for 30% of the NSA's total volume, and may well overtake water filtration sales in the next two or three years. An independent research study by Euromonitor projects a £200 m – £300 m a year market in the UK by 1994.

Many NSA distributors have found that households buying a water system have gone on to buy more than one air filter, so that a number of rooms can be kept odour and dust free. There is a bulk market for offices which exceeds demand for water treatment.

Best estimates from experience so far are that the market may eventually be 3–4 times greater than for water. Whatever the figure, NSA's decision to enter the market at least doubles the earnings opportunity for any NSA distributor.

To an objective observer, everything in this analysis has has been positive: the products have sales features of unique appeal in a hot market, and are priced to sell.

The final question is: are they priced for profit?

Or to put it more bluntly: what's in it for you?

How air filters work

A "micron" is the unit used to measure dirt particles in the air. It is one-millionth of a meter. About 400 would fit on the dot of this letter i.

All bacteria, insecticide dust, animal dander, and smoke particles, are smaller than a micron. So NSA had to find a filtration system that would be effective down to these microscopic levels.

The small-unit filters collect anything larger than 0.3 microns. For the large-room or office filters, NSA went even further. They use what is known as HEPA filtration ("High Efficiency Particulate Air"), which is effective to 0.1 microns.

This filter, developed by the US military, and used by the Atomic Energy Commission for removing radioactive dust from underground sites, cleans air to the standards required by hospital operating theatres and burns units. (You need an electron microscope to see a particle as small as 0.1 micron in size; even viruses are generally larger than this).

Chapter 9

Anyone can do it

There are NSA distributors earning £100,000 a year and more – and they still don't understand all the complexities of the Marketing Plan.

It is a subtle document whose purpose is to match reward with effort. Those who do the most, earn the most. To make sure this happens, NSA has a company policy of learning from experience. Over the years since it adopted network marketing it has regularly updated the Marketing Plan – and will continue to do so, to make sure that its product continues to find end-users, and its independent distributors all have an equal chance of becoming wealthy.

But the bottom line is very simple. Everyone starts as a dealer. Then there is a ladder – or staircase – which can be climbed. Each step brings greater rewards, which come as a combination of discounts, commissions, and bonuses. The top position you can reach is National Marketing Director:

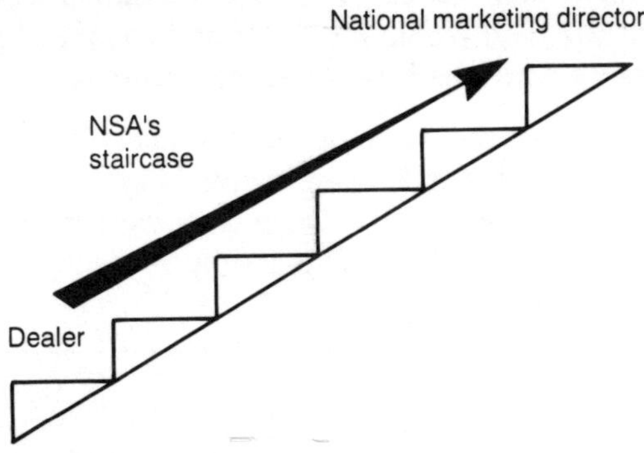

Provided you keep going, it is not hard to move upwards. It is just a question of keeping on retailing, and steadily building your network, so that the monthly turnover of your group grows ever larger. Those who are best at this, and do it consistently, find promotion happens as a matter of course.

The good thing is:

* All positions are permanent

Which means that going up the staircase is not like walking on a treadmill. Move up to any position (at the beginning, you can sometimes manage two steps at a time) and you will never move down. You can take a break for a month, or six months – or forever, if you want to retire – and you will still be eligible to qualify for exactly the same bonuses and commissions that you have earned through your most recent promotion.

When you go to an Evaluation Meeting (so-called because it gives you a chance to evaluate NSA's business, and decide whether it suits you), the Marketing

THE BUILDING SITE

Most people drop out of network marketing in the first few weeks (or sometimes months) because they find things are going too slowly for them. But in a way, building a business is like building a skyscraper.

Think how many times you've walked past a city centre building site, and wondered for months what is going on the other side of the hoardings, apart from noise.

Then, one day, the structure of the first floor emerges. And within weeks it is many storeys high. The foundations are the key to this. Once they are firmly in place, one floor rises quickly above another – each duplicating the one below.

Plan is presented in some detail. Also available, later on, are seminars and refresher sessions which deal with the subtleties of the Plan, and how to use them in building your business.

Right now, if you're thinking of getting started, the main questions are: what can you expect to achieve, and what will it take to get there?

Three types

The short answer is that you can reach the sky, if you set your goal that high and you focus yourself on reaching it. But I found, when I went round NSA's meetings and talked to people who had been in the business for a while, that there seemed to be three broad categories of ambition.

I should stress that these are personal impressions, and that any indications of earnings are not endorsed by NSA, which is rightly cautious of giving people false expectations. Also, people move from one category into another as they learn more about themselves and what they are capable of achieving. On the other hand, it is a fact of life that some people simply give up. The spectrum in network marketing is as wide as in the population as a whole, from non-achievers to millionaires.

But, working from the bottom of the staircase to the top, these are the three general kinds of active, satisfied business builders I came across:

* Part-timers working as dealers/distributors
* Middle management types, usually part-time and hoping to go full-time
* High flyers, giving total attention to the future of their groups

Dealers and distributors

This group consists of people who want some form of secondary income, without too much effort or responsibility for building a business. Retailing is the main activity, much of it happening at the weekend. People start off with two, three or four demonstration water filtration units, and the same number of air filters, to lend out. Working through their list of contacts, it takes them half an hour or so at each visit to fit a unit, and show its benefits.

A week later they go back to get a reaction. Perhaps a third to a half of people want to buy. Almost everyone gives the names of some friends who might be also be interested. These names form the basis of the next series of visits. Week after week, the process continues.

For a few hours spent working on Saturdays and Sundays, these dealers/distributors find themselves clocking up two or three sales a week. The income is not at all bad. Two sales a week of the 100S create a profit of £5,800 per year. Four sales a week, with the added rebates from greater volume, bring in £12,700.

PUPPY-DOGS

When the 50C water filtration demonstration model was introduced in the United States, it had an instant effect on sales. One of the distributors reported back to NSA's head office:

It was like lending someone a puppy-dog for a week. They couldn't bear the thought of handing it back.

The phrase caught on. Within NSA, the 50C is now universally referred to as a "puppy". In marketing terms, it establishes need: people don't realize how much they have missed the taste of clean water, until they get the chance to try it for themselves.

Network builders

This group is probably in the majority. They have grasped the concept of network marketing. They realise that retailing is important, but not the be-all-and-end-all. They go through all the steps outlined earlier in this book, and learn a lot more besides. They find that retailing and sponsoring overlap so much that they are inseparable. Gradually – or quite quickly if they find the right people early on – their networks grow.

I met such a wide variety of people in this group that it is extremely difficult to give guidelines on just how much can be achieved by when. Providing the fundamental teaching attitudes have been laid down properly from the beginning, there seems to be a general take-off point when a network becomes 30–40 strong. To get to this point can take 60 days, 90 days, six months – even a year.

The earnings band is very wide, too. It depends on the mix between retailing and network performance, and – because of the fitfulness of human nature – it varies from month to month. But once you have reached the 30+ level, income should be comfortably more than from retailing alone: the two combined will bring, say, £1,500 to £3,000 per month.

High flyers

This group consists almost entirely of people who are committed full-time (although people's definition of full-time can vary from 25 to 50 or more hours per week). Most of their effort is spent working in depth with their groups, helping to sponsor, constantly explaining and teaching, adding new legs when one of their downlines has become self-replicating.

The more successful they become, the more in demand they are as speakers and trainers at NSA meetings. They find this worthwhile because, by now, their groups have grown to such a size that it is impossible to know everyone personally. A public platform is the only way of getting their teaching message across.

If you want to join this category of earners, your first aim, financially, is to get your group turnover to the point where you qualify to earn through an additional generation. Once you have done this, you will find there is an immediate jump in income: perhaps double what you were earning before.

After that, there is the final step on the staircase to take, which is for NSA to appoint you...

National Marketing Director

You have to have had a mature business going for at least six months, with consistently good performance, before NSA will promote you. The company carefully examines the structure of your network, to see if it is solidly built, and will generate income in the coming years.

The benefits are substantial. They include private health insurance, and a private education allowance. Expenses of up to £21,600, incurred in developing your business, are met. Additionally, NSA may include you in their profit sharing scheme, and in the share allocation which is planned for staff, management, and NMDs in the coming years.

Newly qualified National Marketing Directors (NMDs) are probably all making profits at the rate of £100,000+ a year, and can go on to make many times this amount. There is no set timetable for reaching these giddy heights. A very few have made it within a year; two years is more usual; and it can be a lot longer. The chart on page 88 shows some average figures for what a number of NMDs have found possible.

In 1991 in the UK, about 30 people were appointed as NMDs, bringing the total to more than 50. People coming newly into NSA sometimes look at this figure, relatively small as it is compared with the thousands who register as dealers each year, and find the prospect of becoming an NMD too daunting. They needn't. As with everything in network marketing, it's just a question of numbers and time.

It's best to look at the US for what will most likely happen here. The figures are for water treatment units only. In America, after six years' trading, market penetration is about 5%, and the volume of business has generated 500 NMDs. This is expected to grow to at least 25% penetration and 2,500 NMDs by the end of the decade.

Here, after three years, market penetration is less than 2%. Penetration of 25% would call for at least 500 NMDs in the UK alone – and 4,500 NMDS in the European market as a whole.

It's up to you. It's your business, your time, your effort, your desire.

FOUR GOLDEN RULES

Paula Pritchard is an outstandingly successful NMD in America, who came across to the UK in 1988 to start NSA's operation over here. She has distilled her teaching methods into four golden rules:

TWO WAYS TO SUCCEED

1. Show the product
2. Show the business

TWO WAYS TO FAIL

3. Don't do (1) and (2).
4. Be worried about the outcome of (1) and (2).

IT'S THAT SIMPLE

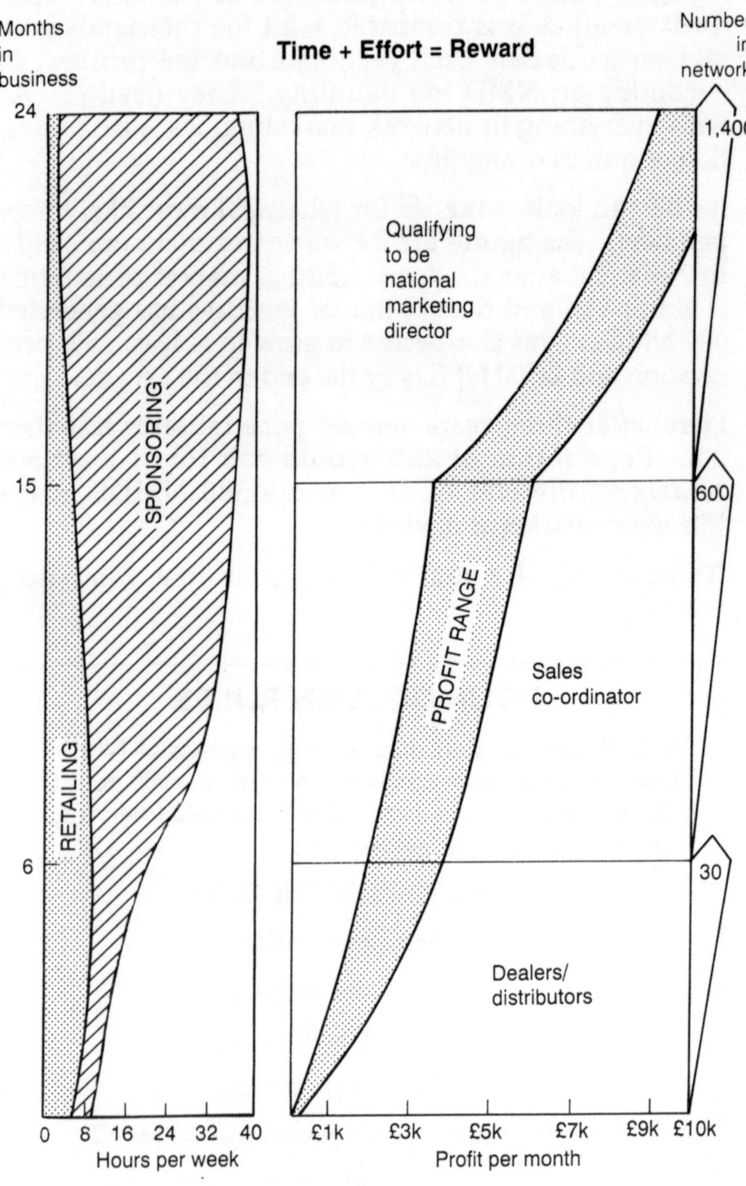
Months
in
business
Time + Effort = Reward
Number
in
network
24
15
6
0
8
16
24
32
40
Hours per week
RETAILING
SPONSORING
Qualifying
to be
national
marketing
director
PROFIT RANGE
Sales
co-ordinator
Dealers/
distributors
1,400
600
30
£1k
£3k
£5k
£7k
£9k
£10k
Profit per month

Chapter 10

Future trends

What we have here is a happy union of a number of powerful business trends.

Whether you look at the growth of network marketing in the UK, or at sales of water and air treatment units in the UK, or at NSA's recent achievement as a company, the pattern is the same. You see consistent growth on a rapidly ascending curve:

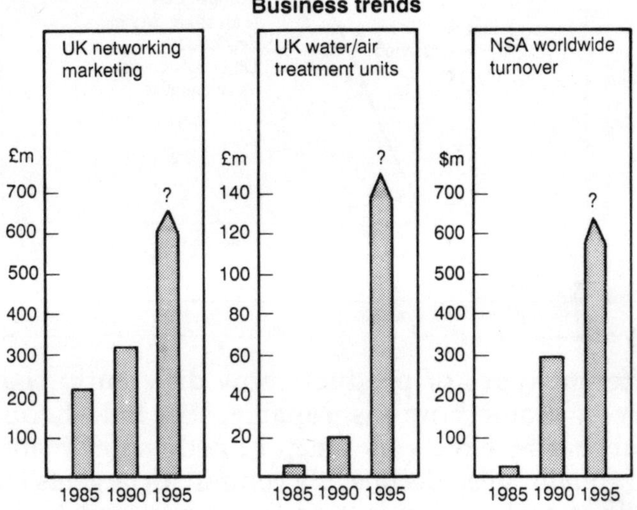

It is this combination of recession-defying statistics which, above all, has persuaded so many people that this is an opportunity not to be missed. The estimated figures for 1995 are projections which I have carefully drawn from past performance, and from sources independent of NSA.

Like all forecasts, the precise figures should be treated with caution. But the trend is unmistakeable. Network marketing is booming; the market for environmental products is booming; NSA is booming.

But how long will it last? To make an informed judgment, there is a standard business concept which you can use: the product life cycle. Any product has a life which mimics the life of a human being. It is introduced to the world, it grows, it reaches maturity, and eventually it declines and dies. In graph form, it can be shown as a curve:

Product life cycle

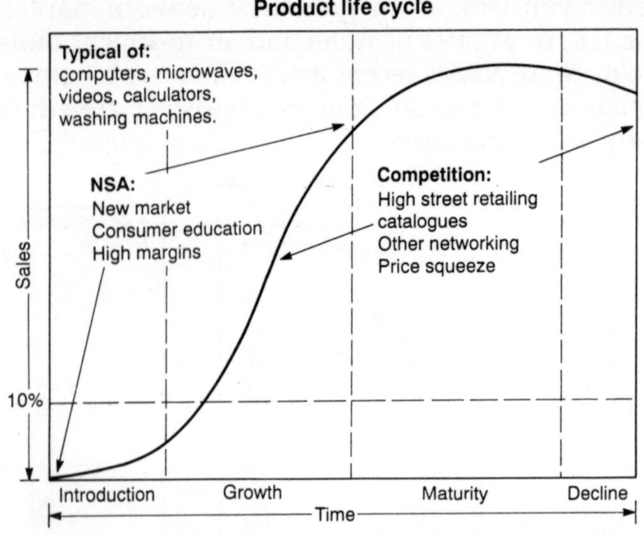

Different types of product show differently shaped curves. Something fashionable, like hula-hoops or skateboards, have very steep growth, short maturity, and equally steep decline. By contrast, detergents took a while to make an impact on the market, but (until oil runs out) are spending a long time in maturity. The curve illustrated is typical of that for household appliances.

There are two important points here. The first is that there is a key breakthrough figure of 10% market penetration. Once this is reached, word-of-mouth and copy-your-neighbour takes over, and the growth curve turns steeply upward.

The second point is that NSA, historically, has operated in the first two stages of the product life cycle. It did so successfully with fire extinguishers, and repeated the process first with water treatment units, second with air filters, and now (in the US) with pre-school learning. New lines of product now being researched and developed are almost certain to fit into the same stage of the cycle.

This strategy is at the same time tough but profitable. It is tough because at the beginning of the cycle, there is low public awareness of the product, or the need for it – which is why NSA distributors lend out their products on a *try it, you'll like it* basis, to get buyers used to the idea.

It is profitable because at this stage the competition is less fierce. Large corporations and retail chains are structured, on the whole, to await public demand, not lead it. Then they move in, and tend to drive prices down. Most of the older multi-level marketing companies, like Amway, operate in the mature stage of the cycle.

For the moment, forget about the air market and other products which NSA will be introducing, and just concentrate on what will probably happen with water filtration. There is a comparison here with microwave ovens.

There are 23 million homes in Britain. Ten years ago, less than 5% had microwaves. At that time, would you have had the vision to predict how quickly they would catch on? When every kitchen already had an oven, and a microwave cost £250–£500? But now, 46% of homes have them.

After a slow beginning, they hit the magic market penetration figure of 10%. And then they took off.

With water filtration units, we are where microwaves were 10 years ago. Less than 2% of homes have them. The number of distributors in NSA, whose effort is creating the market in the UK, is growing fast. In the short to medium term, penetration will be 5%, and then 10% – and then lift-off.

Many NSA distributors – those who have been active for a couple of years – already have networks turning over £100,000 – £1,000,000 per month. But imagine how much money a group you yourself have created will be turning over each month when the 10% figure is reached, and households are coming to you spontaneously asking for water units, instead of you having to tell them how they work.

As Derek Ross, one of NSA's most successful National Marketing Directors, has put it:

I am absolutely sure in my own mind that the person in this country who, in the end, will be NSA's biggest earner, hasn't yet joined the company.

The time to start putting this group in place is surely right now. Very few people – two or three out of a hundred – ever have the vision to spot a trend. NSA is handing you several on a plate: first water, then air, then education, then products you haven't even thought of. It is NSA's job to anticipate the future.

As a business concept, network marketing is growing so fast that, quite soon, you and your friends will almost certainly be approached by other companies with other environmental products. NSA's advantage is that they are already in place, ahead of the growth to come. And you have the bonus of knowing that the company's background is solid, with excellent training facilities for you and those you introduce.

Boom business trends are unstoppable. With or without you, they are going to happen.

Appendix

These facts about a selection of network marketing (or "multi-level marketing") companies have been compiled following a standard telephoned questionnaire to each of the companies early in 1992. So as not to discriminate between them, they are in alphabetical order.

AMWAY

Estimated retail value of sales worldwide has risen from $2 billion in 1989 to $3.3 billion in 1991. In the UK over the same period, sales have increased from £10.5 million to £30 million. About 45,000 UK distributors – half women, half men – are registered on the computer.

The product line has become increasingly varied and extensive. Sales are still dominated by the traditional range of consumables: household cleaners and personal care items. Sales of durable products from a lengthy catalogue now account for about 15% of the total.

About 60% of sales are estimated to go to end-users outside the distributor network. The market advantage is said to be the size and success of the corporation, the breadth of its products, and its "green" image – Amway won a United Nations environmental award in 1989.

Start-up costs are £60 for a distributor pack that includes a personal organizer, 2 videos, and a sample of products. The company claims that it offers its distributors larger commissions over more levels than most other networking companies. It says "about a dozen" people are earning more than £100,000 a year, and that the marketing plan is structured so that the majority of part-timers can expect £12,000 – £20,000 a year.

FIZZ-WIZZ
A company which began to use network marketing in June 1991, and was bought out by its management in December 1991. No sales or turnover figures given. Has approximately £2m in assets, and its own manufacturing base. It reports having 1,500 distributors.

Its product is an electronic carbonated drinksmaker, selling for £99.00 plus VAT, using Corona concentrates as flavourings. Water filtration can be plumbed in as an add-on. Its market advantage is in a cheaper cost-per-drink, compared with cans or bottles, and convenience. Repeatability is from re-orders of gas and concentrates.

Start-up costs for a new distributors are a £25 joining fee, plus wholesale purchase of as little or as much product as required.

HERBALIFE
US parent company formed in 1980. Operates internationally with organisations in France and Spain said to be "ten times larger than in the UK". No UK trading figures provided. Claims 23,000 UK distributors, of whom 60% are active, with more women than men.

The product line consists primarily of diet formulas, said to help weight loss by providing a "full, satisfying feeling". Other products offer nutritional supplements, herbal skin care preparations, and a water filtration unit. The market advantage is claimed to be the advanced scientific formulae, and successful use by many thousands of people.

New distributors buy a start-up pack for £55. A "handful" of people in the UK are earning in the top bracket, in excess of £75,000 a year. The marketing plan encourages part-timers to earn £10,000 a year upwards.

KLEENEZE HOMECARE
After 70 years' trading, Kleeneze's parent company is the only UK network marketing company with a Stock Exchange listing. The group capitalization is above £50 million. No figures for the networking operation released, but sales are said to have increased by 70% in the last 12 months. 3,500 distributors, 65% of them men, but new registrations running at nearer 50/50.

There are 350 products in Kleeneze's catalogue, with the concentration of sales still in the homecare and cleaning categories. The market advantage is said to be the convenience of doorstep deliveries, unconditional guarantees, and a range of products, including specialist clean ers, which cannot be bought elsewhere.

Start-up costs for a new distributor are £70. Company policy not to indicate earnings at any level, because "too many people are misled by statements of high earnings".

L'AROME

A UK company, formed in August 1987. Since then it claims uninterrupted growth, with more than £100m in total sales to December 1991. Major financial restructuring, including liquidation of part of the company, during 1991. During its four years it says it has handled more than 200,000 distributors, of whom currently there are about 40,000 active.

The initial product line was perfumes, to which were added skin-care preparations, and lately a diet plan. The market advantage for perfumes is price, at roughly one-third High Street equivalent; and for the newer lines, careful targeting of niche markets. All products are consumable, and therefore repeatable.

Start-up costs are £15 to a maximum of £75. L'Arome reported one individual £1m earner in a single year (after 4 years building a network), with more than 50 earning more than £100,000, and "hundreds" making £50–£100,000.

NATIONAL SAFETY ASSOCIATES (NSA)

US parent company, with 4,000% growth worldwide in 5 years (from $9m in 1987 to $364m in 1991). UK trading figures follow a similar pattern: 1989, £2.8m; 1990, £14.9m; 1991, £19.3m. Unlike other companies questioned, these figures are wholesale values, net of all commissions. To make them comparable with retail figures otherwise reported, they should probably be multiplied by at least 2.

At the end of 1991, NSA had about 3,000 active direct distributors in the UK, and about 30,000 dealers working through them. About 60% were men.

NSA's product line consists of in-home filtration systems for water and air, selling for approximately £40–£400. The market advantage for the water filters is a price of less than 1p per litre compared with about 40p for bottled water of the same quality; for air, an innovative patented filtration system claimed to be the best in the world.

Start-up costs for a new dealer are a £15 registration fee, plus wholesale purchase of as little or as much product as required. Company policy not to disclose individual earnings.

NATURE'S SUNSHINE PRODUCTS

A 20-year-old US-owned company operating worldwide, sales internationally total $80–85 million per year. UK sales figures are not given, but are said to have been on a continuous growth trend since the launch here in 1989. 4,000 distributors reported, with "44–47% active and regularly placing orders through the company".

The product consists of herbal capsules used widely in alternative medicine. The market advantage, according to the company, is that the product works therapeutically. "It was a successful retail product, and we went into network marketing to reach a larger number of consumers."

Startup costs are £50–£100. A few top earners, after two years in the business, are making £6–£7,000 a month.

NUTRI-METRICS

Started in the US 30 years ago, pioneering vitamin additives and health foods. Turnover in the UK in mid-1991 was less than £1m annually, and declining. The trend was reversed when taken over by Roche, Australia's largest direct-sales cosmetics company. Currently, there are about 750 UK distributors, of whom 95% are women.

The product line now concentrates on organic skin care, using treatments not tested on animals. The market advantage is said to be quality.

New distributors start up with an initial product order of £69.95. After less than a year under the new regime, there are no big-time earners yet. The company hopes that some of its most successful distributors will soon be earning £3,000 – £4,000 a month.